The Loneliest Journey

The Loneliest Journey

SHEILA CASSIDY

First published in 1995 by
Darton, Longman and Todd Ltd
1 Spencer Court
140–142 Wandsworth High Street
London SW18 4JJ

ISBN 0–232–52120–4

A catalogue record for this book is available
from the British Library

Acknowledgement is due to Orbis Books for the poem 'Go
Down' by Helder Camara, from his book *The Desert is Fertile*.
Originally published as *Le Désert est Fertile* by Desclée de Brouwer.
Translated by Dinah Livingstone. English translation copyright
© 1974 Orbis Books, Maryknoll, New York 10545.

Phototypeset in 11/13pt Bembo by Intype, London
Printed and bound in Great Britain by
Page Bros, Norwich

This book is dedicated in love and gratitude to:

Colin, Joanna, John, Peggy, Steve and Sue
who battle with cancer as I write

Barbara, Chris, David, Jackie and Sue
and my other colleagues in the Plymouth Oncology Unit

David, Malin and Rebecca
whose friendship has enriched my life beyond measure

Acknowledgements

My thanks are due to all who have made this book possible; to Morag Reeve of Darton, Longman and Todd, whose encouragement I find invaluable, to Angela Tilby, Carolyn Brodribb, Vivienne Seymour Clark, Gerry Hughes and David Lobb who have advised me on various parts of the manuscript, to my colleagues in the Mustard Tree Cancer Support Centre who have been endlessly patient while I have been preoccupied with writing and lastly to Barbara, my secretary, who has worked so hard and so willingly in the typing and preparation of the manuscript.

Introduction

This is the story of the loneliest journey of our lives, the journey which takes us through the 'dark valley' of illness and fear to the gates of death. It is not the story of a 'real' individual, of Tom or Jane or Mary, but that does not mean it is not a true story. Everything that happens in this narrative has happened to someone, and each person who speaks is 'real' in the sense that they have been forged out of fragments of men and women who live or have lived on this planet. This, then, is a story about people, well people who become sick, and sick people who become well again, and the men and women who care for them as best they can. Some of my characters are cured of their illness, some conquer it for a time, whilst others die quite soon. As I said before, this is a true story, and this is the way things are.

My story has a purpose in that it seeks to be the voice of those men and women who battle so bravely with one of the nastiest diseases to which humankind is heir. If, by revealing some of their pain, their fear and their anger I can deepen the insight and understanding of the families, friends and carers of future cancer sufferers, then this book will have been worth the writing.

Among 'those who battle' I include the 'professionals', those skilled or not so skilled men and women who, for whatever reason, have chosen to work in the field of cancer care. I have 'drawn' them both at work and at home, revealing them in all their vulnerability, not because I wish to 'expose' them but because I wish to make it clear that they, too, are ordinary men and women, prey to precisely the same weaknesses and temptations as their patients.

The 'patients' in my story are men and women with cancer, because this is the disease with which I am most familiar. Many of the emotions, however, are universal, meaning they are experienced by anyone who suddenly finds themselves struck down by serious illness. There is, I believe, a particular similarity between all the diseases which are known to be progressive and potentially fatal: cancer, motor neurone disease and AIDS, although the latter illness has the added and devastating complication of social ostracism.

Let me begin my story where most of us begin; as normal, healthy human beings who do not expect to get seriously ill and who, absurdly, do not really expect to die. Assuming that we are going to live for ever, or rather, forgetting that we are going to die is one of life's great *coping strategies*; we know, intellectually, that a certain proportion of the population will have car accidents, drown at sea, fall down mountains, or get cancer, but, secretly, we always think that this will happen to the other man or woman. We know, too, that we shall get older and stiffer and gradually more frail; we arrange pensions for our old age and take out life insurance policies to support our dependants in case we die, but I suspect that, deep in our hearts we don't think that this will happen to *us*. This book then, is an attempt to show that 'no man is an island', that those we happily think of as *them* are, in reality, *us*.

At the back of the book is an appendix of comments on each chapter. These are intended for students of cancer care in particular and for anyone who is interested in exploring the experience of the characters in greater depth.

SHEILA CASSIDY, 1995

1

Mary Carlisle was just 40 on the day she discovered the cancer in her breast. One minute she was lying happily in the bath, looking forward to her birthday dinner, the next, she was grappling with a wild terror; there was a lump in her breast. Drugged by the heat of the water and the smell of bath essence, Mary's brain was slow to realise the significance of what her fingers had found. Suddenly, the knowledge hit her and she sat up abruptly and felt the breast again. She must be mistaken, dear God, let it be a mistake . . . but no, there was a hard irregular lump about the size of an acorn.

Mary felt sick, very sick, and wondered if she would throw up in the bath. She felt cold, too, and a bit dizzy as she climbed out of the bath to confront her terrified face in the mirror. Educated at a convent school, Mary had never been completely at home with the sight of her naked body, but, struggling to regain her composure, she looked hard at her breasts in the large bathroom mirror. At first it seemed that there was nothing amiss, but when she put her hands together behind her head she could see that the two breasts were slightly different. There was an unusual fullness just above the nipple on the left side.

Mary's throat constricted and she wanted to scream. Her mind ran amok. Cancer, she thought. Mastectomy. Mutilation. Pain. Death. John, she thought. Where was John? She needed him. Where was he? She tried to call out for her husband but the words stuck in her throat and she gave only a pitiful, strangled cry. Picking up her towel from the floor she wrapped herself in its warm folds and, struggling to pull herself together, sat down on the lavatory seat to think.

'Calm down, Mary,' she heard herself saying. 'You're out of control.' Taking some deep breaths she tried to think clearly. She should call John. He'd know what to do. They should call the doctor right away . . . she paused and realised that she was getting carried away. Whatever was wrong with her breast it was not an

1

emergency. It could wait till the morning. John . . . she thought desperately.

She opened her mouth to call him . . . and then closed it again. Poor John. He'd be so worried. It would spoil the entire evening. It wouldn't be fair. Anyway, she reasoned, perhaps it was nothing. Perhaps it would go away. It was probably mastitis or something to do with her periods. Briefly, she felt reassured; but then the icy cold fear in her heart returned and she knew it is something serious.

Clear minded at last, she formulated her plan. She would *not* tell John tonight. She would do her best to be light-hearted for his sake, and tomorrow she would make an appointment to see the doctor. *Que sera, sera*, she mused. Whatever will be will be. The following day, however, Mary could not bring herself to phone the surgery. 'I'll wait till after my next period', she told herself, 'and see if it goes away. I'm probably making a fuss about nothing.'

Two weeks passed and Mary's period came and went. John, noticing that she was more edgy than normal, put it down to the vagaries of the female state and wondered if it could possibly be the change of life.

Each night in the bath Mary examined the lump. At least it doesn't hurt, she thought. It can't be anything serious if it doesn't hurt. When three weeks have elapsed, John went North on a short business trip and Mary decided that this was the time to see the doctor. Accordingly she booked the earliest appointment that she could get without making a fuss and tried to compose herself in patience to wait.

Dr Michael Howard looked at his watch and sighed. It was one o'clock and he was due at the hospital before two. Damn, he thought. Another day with no lunch. I wish they wouldn't book me so many patients. Wearily he pressed the intercom. 'Mrs Carlisle, please.'

Michael looked up at the pale woman who entered the surgery. Carlisle. Mary. Of course, mother of Lisa and Jamie. What could be the matter with her? He hoped it was nothing gynaecological because he certainly hadn't got time to examine her. Michael managed a brief smile. 'Hello,' he said. 'What can I do for you?'

2

Mary sat in her chair looking down at her hands and twisting her handkerchief between her fingers. Blast! thought Michael . . . this is not going to be a quickie. Struggling to keep his irritation under control he said again, 'What seems to be the problem, Mrs Carlisle?'

Picking up the tone of irritation in his voice, Mary opened her mouth and then shut it again. Oh God, was she making a fuss about nothing? 'I'm sorry,' she said at last. 'I'm probably being stupid. I expect it's nothing, but, but, I've been a bit worried. You see, I've found a lump in my breast.'

Michael cursed silently to himself. He glanced covertly at his watch. It was ten past one. He mustn't be late again. Standing up, he said to Mary, 'Shall we have a look at it then. Could you pop behind the curtain, please, and slip your top things off?'

Mary retreated behind the curtain and fumbled with her blouse. Michael sat down heavily in his chair and tried not to be irritated by the length of time it was taking the woman to undress.

It's not my day, he thought ruefully, and his mind went back to the tense scene at breakfast when his wife had burst into tears because he'd snapped at her for burning the toast. Oh God, he thought, what's going wrong with us? We used to be so happy.

Michael was so deep in his thoughts that he hardly heard Mary's faint, 'I'm ready doctor.'

He went behind the curtain to find Mary stripped to the waist, lying down on the examination couch. 'Could you sit up please.' He knew his voice was not as gentle as it should have been. He looked carefully at the two breasts and, noting the fullness in the left one, put his hand straight on to the lump. Damn, he thought. Poor bloody woman. He looked briefly at her face as he examined the other breast. She looked terrified.

Michael knew he ought to talk to Mary, but there was just no time. Better reassure her and make an appointment at the hospital. After all, it *could* be benign.

'That's fine, Mrs Carlisle,' he said briskly. 'Just slip your things on again, would you?'

Mary looked at the doctor's back as he disappeared quickly behind the curtain. She wanted to scream at him, Well? What do you think? Is it cancer? Is it? Slowly, she put on her clothes again and returned to her seat in front of the doctor's desk. He was writing a letter and did not look up at her for what seemed an eternity. When he did look up, she tried to read his face but couldn't. It was as though his eyes were shutters, concealing his thoughts from her.

'Now, Mrs Carlisle,' he said, 'I'm sure there's nothing to worry about, but I'll arrange for you to see Mr Dalton at the hospital for a few tests. It'll take a couple of weeks. Goodbye now. Try not to worry about it.' Michael picked up his briefcase and, holding the door for Mary, followed her out into the corridor.

The waiting room was empty and there was no one at the receptionist's counter. Mary, realising that she was the last patient of the morning sat down heavily on one of the moulded plastic chairs and began to cry. She had not slept properly for the past three weeks, and, having steeled herself to face the doctor she was overcome by a sense of anticlimax and impotence. There had been so many questions that she had wanted to ask him. Did the doctor think it was cancer? What were her chances? What was the treatment? Would she have to have a mastectomy? Would that cure it? What about drugs treatment? Was it really as terrible as people said?

The tears rolled down her cheeks unheeded and she gave way to despair. She couldn't even remember what the doctor had said about the specialist. Had he said that he would make the appointment, or had he told her to? For the life of her she couldn't remember. She felt unbelievably stupid and confused and her tears fell more heavily than ever. At last, pulling herself together, Mary blew her nose, and went into the ladies' room to wash her face.

Practice nurse Caroline Sheldon put the lid back on her plastic lunch box and said, 'Well! I don't know about you Annie, but I feel a lot better!' Annie, the district nurse licked the jam from a half-eaten doughnut off her lips and said, 'I don't know how you survive on all that rabbit food, Caroline. I should die of hunger.'

Caroline grinned. 'But I had a yogurt too, Annie,' she said. 'I'm positively full.'

'How about some coffee,' said Annie, who knew her friend far too well to rise to the bait.

Caroline, who was a good natured energetic woman in her early forties, sprang to her feet. Taking the electric jug she made her way to the staff washroom to refill it. As she passed the patients' toilet she heard a muffled sob and, pushing the swing door she saw a woman of her own age desperately trying to wash away the traces of a heavy bout of crying.

'Hello,' said Caroline. 'Are you all right?'

Mary looked up at Caroline's trim figure, and noting the nurse's uniform felt a fleeting sense of relief. 'I'm sorry,' she said, 'but I just can't stop crying. I'm probably being awfully stupid, but I'm just so frightened.' Mary gulped and once again the tears overcame her and as Caroline stepped towards her, she moved into the other woman's arms and found herself being held like a child.

Caroline held Mary firmly for a few moments, then, sliding her arm around the weeping woman's shoulders, led her along the corridor to her own small room. Settling her down in an easy chair, Caroline said quietly, 'I was just making some coffee. Would you like some?' Mary nodded her head. 'Yes please,' she said. 'Milk, but no sugar.' Caroline smiled. 'You just sit there,' she said, 'and I'll be back in a minute or two.'

Caroline returned to the staff room and plugged in the kettle. 'What kept you?' said Annie, who liked her lunch time coffee hot on the heels of whatever sweet confectionery was her indulgence for the day.

'I found a woman crying in the loo,' she said. 'Sobbing her heart out.'

'What about?' said Annie with interest.

'I don't know yet,' said Caroline. 'I'm about to go and find out.'

They sat in silence until the kettle boiled and Caroline had made three mugs of coffee. Annie heaved herself to her feet to open the door for her friend. 'Let me know if there's anything I can do,' she said. 'I'll be around for about an hour and then I've got a whole string of visits.'

'Thanks,' said Caroline. 'I'll let you know.'

Caroline listened quietly while, falteringly, Mary told her how she had found the lump and of her fears that it was cancer. Caroline was silent for a few moments, waiting to see if Mary had anything else to say, then, she asked quietly, 'What did Dr Howard say when he examined you?'

'He hardly said anything.' said Mary. 'I suppose that's part of

5

my trouble. There were so many things I needed to ask him, but he was so busy and I was so confused that I didn't dare.'

Caroline sighed to herself. These bloody doctors, always in such a hurry. It never seems to occur to them that women with breast lumps are practically paralysed with fear. Why couldn't he have asked one of us to see her, to explain things a bit, if he hadn't got the time?

Caroline took a deep breath. 'Doctor Howard's doing a clinic at the hospital this afternoon,' she said. 'He'll probably have got there by now. Would you like me to give him a quick phone call and ask him if he'd like me to explain things to you a bit?'

Mary looked scared. 'Won't he be cross?' she said. 'He'll think I'm making a fuss.'

Caroline seethed internally. Poor bloody woman. Making a fuss indeed! When she's just discovered she's probably got cancer and that maybe she's going to die. 'Not at all,' said Caroline. 'It'll be no problem. I'll just give him a ring.'

Michael arrived at the Out Patient Department just on two o'clock and, escaping the eagle eye of the Out Patient Sister, ensconced himself in the consulting room. Pam, the nurse who ran the clinic grinned at him. 'Relax,' she said. 'The first patient's only just got here and she's being weighed at the moment. And, there's a message from the surgery'. She searched in her pocket for a scrap of paper. 'Could you ring Caroline as soon as you get here?' Michael's blood pressure rose a fraction. What could Caroline want? Surely, it couldn't be an emergency. Bob, the senior partner was on call for the afternoon. He dialled the surgery and asked to speak to her.

Caroline took a deep breath. Michael's voice was terse and she knew she must tread gently. 'I'm sorry to bother you,' she said, 'but it's about Mrs Carlisle, the lady you saw this morning.'

'Yes,' said Michael. 'What about her? I've arranged for her to see Mr Dalton next week. Is there some problem?'

Caroline took the plunge. 'It's just that she's very distressed,' she said calmly, 'and she has a lot of questions she needs to ask.' Michael knew he'd been too quick with her and guilt made him irritable. 'I'm sorry, Caroline,' he said. 'She'll have to make another appointment. There's nothing I can do about it now.'

6

Caroline cut in quickly, before he could put the phone down on her. 'Would you mind if I looked at your notes and had a talk with her myself?' she asked. 'You know I'm doing this counselling course and . . .'

Michael sighed with relief that Caroline was not expecting him to do anything about the woman himself. 'Of course not,' he said. 'They're on my desk unless Molly has cleared them away. There's a letter to the surgeon. You'd better have a look at that too.'

'Thank you very much,' said Caroline and put the phone down thankfully.

'A bit tetchy today aren't we?' said Annie who had been listening to Caroline's end of the conversation.

'I don't know what's the matter with him,' said Caroline. 'He's normally really caring and spends hours with people like Mrs Carlisle. Maybe something's wrong at home.'

'Trouble with his marriage,' said Annie gloomily, 'or another woman.'

'Oh shut up, Annie,' said Caroline. 'You've no evidence. That's how rumours start.'

'Sorry,' said Annie, offended, and not a little ashamed of herself. 'Oh Annie! Don't be offended,' said Caroline. 'Will you be around in about half an hour? I don't think this woman's in any state to drive herself home. Could you be an angel . . .'

Annie grinned. 'Okay,' she said. 'It'll be an excuse to sit here and read my stars a bit longer. But don't be too long, I can't wait for ever.'

2

Caroline found Mary's notes easily enough, and noticed that the slim packet had only two sheets in it. Mary was clearly not a frequent visitor to the surgery. Today's notes were brief in the extreme: Three week's lump (L) breast. No pain. O/E/ Hard mass 2cm. Fixed. Axilla: 2 large nodes. R. breast N.A.D. Urgent appt. Letter √. Caroline sighed. How bald the notes were, telling nothing of the three weeks of terror this woman had suffered, nothing of the sleepnessness, the confusion, the diminished sense of self-worth she had suffered.

Conscious that time was passing, Caroline ripped open a brown envelope. Dear Mr Dalton, she read, re Mrs M. Carlisle, 40. Could you please see this woman urgently? Advanced carcinoma left breast with nodes in the axilla. So. There was no doubt in Michael's mind that this was cancer. He just hadn't told Mary. What should *she* do? Should she continue the tone of cheerful optimism which the doctor had set? Or should she tell Mary the truth: that her suspicions were well founded, that there was a definite possibility that she had cancer.

Taking a deep breath, Caroline decided she must play it 'by ear,' respond honestly to Mary's questions without lying on the one hand, or volunteering bad news on the other. She returned to the office and settled down. She looked at Mary and smiled. 'I spoke to Dr Howard,' she said, 'and he's very happy for me to answer any questions you may have as best I can.'

Mary was silent for a moment, then, seeing her notes in Caroline's hand she blurted out, 'Does he think it's cancer? Does he?'

Caroline leaned forward a little. 'I'm sorry, Mary,' she said, 'but it seems that it's a definite possibility.'

Mary sat silently for what seemed an eternity. Caroline longed to rush in with comforting information, not to leave Mary without hope, but she knew she must leave Mary this space to process the information. Sure enough, Mary spoke again. 'So Dr Howard thinks it's cancer,' she said, as if struggling to comprehend a complex problem.

'Yes,' said Caroline. 'He thinks it's cancer. I'm so sorry.'

'Oh God,' said Mary, 'Oh God. What am I going to do?'

This sounded like a rhetorical question, so Caroline waited. Then, gently, she said, 'We won't know for certain till we've done some tests. Dr Howard has arranged for you to see Mr Dalton, one of the surgeons at the hospital.'

'What will he do?' Mary asked. 'Will he have to do a mastectomy? Will I lose my breast?'

Caroline's heart went out to the frightened woman, for she knew that she too would be devastated to lose one of her breasts. 'He'll have to do some tests,' she said. 'A special X-ray called a mammogram and a biopsy.'

'A biopsy?' Mary looked anxiously at her.

'A biopsy is when they take a little bit of tissue away and look at it under the microscope,' said Caroline carefully. How easy it was to forget that non-medical people often didn't understand terms which were so familiar to doctors and nurses.

Mary paused. Then looking at Caroline she asked once more, 'And if the test shows it's cancer, will they . . .' she stumbled . . . 'will they take the breast away?'

Caroline paused for a moment while she thought. The trouble was, she wasn't sure what to say. She knew that the treatment of breast cancer had changed a lot since she was a hospital nurse. In those days, it was routine to perform a radical mastectomy but now such a mutilating operation was rarely performed, because research had shown long term survival was no higher than if only the lump itself was cut out and the patient given radiotherapy. On the other hand, some surgeons still did simple mastectomies . . .

Mary was aware of Caroline's silence and misinterpreted it. 'Oh God,' she said, 'I'm so afraid.'

Putting all technical thoughts of surgery from her mind Caroline returned to cope with Mary's fear. 'What exactly is it you're afraid of, Mary?' She said.

Mary was silent, and Caroline was about to rephrase her question when the woman blurted out, 'I'm afraid he'll leave me; I'm afraid John'll leave me.'

Oh my Lord . . . Caroline wondered what she had got herself into. Slowly, searching desperately for the right turn of phrase and not really finding it, she said, 'Leave you? Why should he leave you?'

Once again, Mary was silent, then looking very embarrassed, she said slowly, 'John, my husband . . . he likes my breasts. When we make love . . .' she paused, too embarrassed to continue, then, with a harsh sob, she cried, 'I'm afraid that if I lose one of my breasts he won't want me any more.'

Caroline knelt beside the weeping woman and putting her arm around Mary's shoulders, she held her firmly until the crying stopped. Then, giving her a handful of tissues, she returned to her seat. What should she say now? How could she reassure her when she didn't even know the man? 'Have you talked to your husband about this,' she asked tentatively. Mary shook her head, but said nothing. 'Does he know you're here?' Caroline said. Mary shook her head again. 'But he knows you've got the lump?' Caroline said, struggling to understand the situation.

Mary was silent for a moment, then she said almost inaudibly, 'No. I didn't want to worry him.'

Caroline was more confused than ever. 'Were you afraid to tell him?' she asked.

Mary shook her head. 'Oh no,' she said. 'I've wanted to tell him ever since I found the lump, but I didn't want to worry him, and, and . . . I kept hoping it might go away.'

'Oh Mary . . .' Caroline found herself standing, as it were, in the terrifying muddle of Mary's mind. It was a world of fear and confusion, of dark shadows and misconceptions. She longed to confide in her husband, desperately needed his help but was so afraid of rejection that she dared not trust him. Her fear and self-doubt had made her cut herself off from the one person who should be supporting her. For a moment, Caroline felt as lost as Mary, then, taking hold of herself, she said firmly, 'You're going to have to tell him now, aren't you Mary?'

Mary nodded. 'He's coming home tonight,' she said. 'I'll tell him tonight. He'll be home around five.'

'Good,' said Caroline, thankfully. 'I'm sure you'll feel better when you've told him.'

Mary smiled weakly. 'I expect you're right,' she said.

Caroline looked at her watch: it was nearly three o'clock and the Antenatal Clinic would be starting any minute. She stood up.

10

'I'll have to go now,' she said. 'How would it be if I asked Annie, our district nurse, to drive you home and then you and John can walk up tonight and pick up the car. I don't think you should really be driving at the moment, you're too shaken.'

Mary looked gratefully up at her. 'Would she really?' she said. 'That would be wonderful. I must admit, I do still feel a bit wobbly.'

Caroline smiled warmly. 'I'm not surprised,' she said. 'You've been to hell and back. I'm sure you'll feel steadier when you've got John's support.'

Mary nodded, 'You've been very kind,' she said.

Crossing her fingers that Annie had been able to wait, Caroline opened the door.

3

The restaurant car was full and John had to wait to use the phone. After what seemed an age he got through: 'Mary? Hello love,' he said, 'I'll be in at five-thirty. Can you pick me up?'

Her voice was strained: 'I can't, she said, 'I haven't got the car.' 'What's the matter?' John tried to keep the irritation out of his voice. 'Have you pranged it?'

'No, I . . . there was a muffled sob and then the line went dead as the train entered a tunnel. John swore. 'Blast, these damn phones never work when you want them too.' He was about to dial again when a voice behind him said, 'Have you finished?'

He swore again quietly to himself, then said politely, 'Sorry, yes, I've finished.' He returned to his seat and picked up his book, but found he couldn't settle to it. What's the matter with her he wondered? What's happened? Then, irritated with himself for worrying, he made another effort and settled down to read.

There was a long queue for the taxis, so it was nearly six by the time John let himself into the house. 'Mary!' he called. 'Are you there?' There was no answer and at first he thought the house must be empty. Where was she, he wondered, and where were the kids? He called again: 'Mary,' and this time there was an answer, a strained voice answering, 'I'm up here, in the bedroom.'

Dropping his coat and briefcase on the floor, John went up the stairs two at a time and pushed open the bedroom door. Mary sat on the end of the bed with her back to him, looking out of the window; her hair was dishevelled and he knew at once that she'd been crying. What on earth's the matter he thought. It's not like Mary to let herself go like this. He felt a cold hand around his heart. The children. Had something happened to the children? He moved quickly to her side and, sitting beside her, took both her hands in his. 'Mary darling, what is it? What's the matter?' Pulling her hands free from his, Mary flung her arms around his neck and began to sob wildly. John held her close to his chest until the sobs quietened. 'Mary,' he said firmly. 'What on earth is the matter? Will you please tell me?'

Mary buried her face deeper still in his chest and then, pulling herself together for a moment said in a halting voice 'The doctor thinks I've got cancer.'

John felt cold inside, icy cold like an empty house in winter, hollow, like a cored out reed. Cancer, he thought. Cancer. It couldn't be true. Not Mary, his Mary. There must be some mistake. Mary still clung to him and he held her tight, burying his face in her hair. When he had regained his equilibrium he said, 'Tell me about it, Mary. When did you see the doctor? What made you go to see him?'

Mary's eyes were full of tears as she faced him. 'Hold my hand,' she said, 'hold me John. Hold me.' Holding her hand tightly, John repeated his question 'Tell me about it, darling. Please.'

When at last Mary found her voice, the words came in a rush: 'It's my breast. I've got a lump in my breast. I found it three weeks ago on my birthday just before we went out to dinner.'

John interrupted her: 'Three weeks ago! Why on earth didn't you tell me?' Mary's voice quavered. 'I didn't want to worry you. I thought maybe it would go away.'

'Oh my darling.' Now it was John's turn to cry. You didn't want to worry me he thought. Oh my God. Mary. My poor brave, stupid Mary. 'Oh Mary,' he said. 'How could you? How could you think I wouldn't want to know, to share it with you?' He paused, then, taking a deep breath. 'Tell me about the doctor. When did you go?'

Haltingly, Mary told him about her visit to the surgery, of her conversation with Dr Howard and how kind Caroline and Annie had been. John listened quietly as she talked, while his heart felt heavier and heavier. It's serious, he thought. He could tell it was serious. They'd never have spent all that time with her if it hadn't been serious. What now?

Then, when it was all out, Mary remembered about the car. 'John,' she said 'The car. It's at the surgery. I said you'd pick it up. I left the keys with the receptionist.'

Still holding Mary's hand, John said quietly: 'What about you? I don't want to leave you.'

'I'll be okay. I promise. You go.' Mary's voice was stronger now. 'Caroline said would you like to see the doctor but, but, I was afraid.'

'Afraid?' John was puzzled.

Mary began to cry again. 'Afraid they'd tell you I wasn't going to get better, that they'd tell you things they wouldn't tell me.'

'Oh my darling. My poor darling Mary. Are you really afraid of that?'

'I don't know John. The doctor looked so serious. I just don't know.'

'Sweetheart.' John took a deep breath. 'Listen to me. You've only just found this lump. You haven't even seen the surgeon yet. You haven't had any tests. Modern treatment is really good – and we'll get the very best. If necessary, we'll go privately, we'll go to London, to America. Anywhere. You're going to be all right. Do you hear me? You're going to be fine. We'll fight this together, you and me. Now, blow your nose. We're going to walk up to the surgery together to fetch the car. The walk will do you good.'

Mary blew her nose hard into John's clean white handkerchief. Thank God for John. He'd look after her. He'd make everything all right.

Caroline was getting ready to go when Mary and John came through the surgery door. She watched quietly as John, Mary's hand held firmly in his, asked the receptionist for the keys to their car. He looks nice, she thought. Thank God she's got him. She's going to need all the support she can get. 'Caroline, are you busy?' Mary was smiling and walking towards her. 'I'd like you to meet my husband. John, this is Caroline.'

John smiled warmly. 'Thank you so much for all you did for Mary this morning. We're *so* grateful.'

Caroline took his outstretched hand and smiled shyly. 'It was no trouble. I'm glad you're home, though. Mary needs you.'

'I know,' said John. 'I'll be around. Don't worry.' Mary gripped his hand again. 'Shall we go?' said John cheerfully. 'Okay. Home James. It's time we had some supper.'

Caroline smiled. 'Goodbye now.' Well done John, she thought. Good luck. It's going to be a long hard road for both of you.

Michael came out of his surgery in time to see John and Mary disappearing out of the surgery door. He looked tired and drawn. 'God, what a day. How'd you get on with Mrs Carlisle?'

'Oh, fine,' said Caroline. 'I just listened to her really. She was so desperate she couldn't take in anything more.'

'There'll be time enough for that,' said Michael. 'How's the husband?'

'I've just met him. He seems really supportive.'

'Thank God for that. Well done, Caroline. Thanks a million.'

'Well,' said Caroline, 'my counselling skills are coming in useful, aren't they?'

'How right you are.' Michael grinned. 'Perhaps I should do a course myself!'

Back in the surgery, Michael sat down to do some dictating. Suddenly he found there were tears in his eyes. Counselling, he thought. He would be better going to marriage guidance to learn how to talk to Jane. Oh God. What's gone wrong? They used to be so happy. Surely there can't be anyone else? He couldn't bear it if there was, just couldn't bear it.

There was a knock on his door and Molly came in with some coffee for him. 'I'm off now, doctor. Anything more you want tonight?'

Michael looked up, startled out of his reverie. 'Nothing thanks,' he said. 'I've just got a bit of dictating to do and then I'll be off home too.'

'How's Jane?' said Molly casually.

Damn, thought Michael. Surely Molly doesn't suspect something's wrong. Michael took a deep breath. 'She's fine, thank you, Molly. Absolutely fine. Good night.'

'Good night, doctor.' Molly retreated, unconvinced. She could have sworn he had been crying and wondered what was up.

John switched off the engine and they sat for a while. 'What about the kids, Mary? What are we going to tell them?'

'Oh John,' she said weakly. 'Do we have to? Couldn't we wait a bit? Wait till I've seen the surgeon?' John was silent. 'Please darling,' she said. 'I couldn't face telling them at the moment. They wouldn't understand. I just couldn't cope.'

John was doubtful. They'll know something's wrong, he thought. They're not daft. Kids have antennae: the pick up the subtlest vibes. He sighed. 'Okay, love,' he said. 'We'll wait. What time do they get home?'

Mary looked at her watch. 'Not till half eight,' she said, 'and then it'll be nearly bed time. They'll be full of their own doings. They won't notice. You'll see.'

John said nothing and they got out of the car and walked together towards the front door.

4

Katie Roberts looked at the doctor in disbelief. 'Cancer', she said. 'You mean I've got cancer?'

'I'm sorry, Mrs Roberts', said gynaecologist Peter Smith. 'But the biopsy we took last week shows that the cells in the neck of the womb are definitely malignant.' Katie sat there stunned. She hadn't bargained for this. Not *this*. Not cancer. What the hell *now*? she thought. What about the kids? Pull yourself together Katie, her inner voice was sharp. Listen to the man. He's talking to you.

'I'm sorry,' she said. 'It's a bit of a shock.'

'I'm so sorry.' The doctor's voice was gentle. Slow down Peter, he told himself. Give the girl some space. She looks punch drunk. Better get one of the nurses to have a talk with her.

'Mrs Roberts . . .' Katie looked up. 'I think you need a bit of time to absorb this news. How would it be if I get one of my nurses to give you a cup of coffee and then when you're feeling better we can talk again. Is your husband with you?'

'I haven't got a husband.' Katie's reply was sharp. 'I'm a single parent.'

Peter was silent. Damn, he thought. Put his foot in it there. How the hell's she going to cope? He hoped to God the support nurse was free – he couldn't handle this one. He stood up and looked at the Clinic nurse standing expectantly in the corner. 'Jean, could you see if Clare is free to talk to Mrs Roberts, please, and I'd like to see her again at the end of the clinic.'

Jean nodded and, taking Katie gently by the arm, led her out of the clinic.

It was just on six o'clock when social worker Sarah Jane Westward's grubby Peugeot 205 skidded to a halt in the hospital car park, its driver cursing herself for being late yet again for her supervision session with psychiatrist Chris Walker. Sarah stood impatiently on the doorstep of the Psychiatric Clinic wondering how it was that some people always managed to be early, while she . . .

Chris grinned as he opened the door. 'It's okay, Sarah, I'm running late too. Relax. Caroline's just rung to say that she's on her way.'

Ten minutes later, the three of them had settled down, coffee in hand, to discuss some of the patients they had seen during the previous two weeks. Sarah glanced at her notes. 'Shall I begin?' she said.

'Fine by me.' Caroline, who hated going first, relaxed visibly.

'Right,' Sarah began, 'I'd like to talk about a lady I saw yesterday in the Gynae Clinic. She's got an early carcinoma of the cervix.'

'So it's potentially cureable?' said Chris.

'We hope so,' said Sarah. She was referred to me by Clare, the Oncology Support Nurse. It turns out she's 29, a single mother, with three kids, all by different fathers . . .'

'How old are the children?' Chris looked up from his notes. 'I was coming to that. The eldest is 13, the middle one five and there's a toddler of 18 months.'

'Any support?' asked Chris, his mind already considering the consequences upon her children of Katie's possible death.

Sarah shook her head, 'None that I can determine. The 13 year old sounds a real little madam, stays out late and so on. Katie just can't handle her. There's a boyfriend but he's just walked out.'

Chris sighed, 'What sort of treatment are they planning?' he said. 'Surgery or radiotherapy?'

'Surgery: they're planning a Wertheim's hysterectomy – removal of the uterus and all the glands. It's a big procedure, not to mention losing her uterus at such an early age.'

'How's she taking it?'

'So so. She's more angry than anything at the moment. Angry with her GP because he didn't diagnose it earlier, angry with her daughter for being no help and angry with her fella who pushed off the moment he found she was ill.'

'How does she feel about having a hysterectomy? Is it going to hit her hard?'

'I don't know. I don't think she's really processed that bit yet. She's still struggling with the fact that she's got cancer. She feels dirty. Contaminated. She can't bear the thought of something so evil growing secretly inside her.'

18

'Poor lady.' Chris looked pensive. 'What about her background? Have you had time to find out where she's come from?'

'Her mother's dead. I've gathered that much. And she hasn't seen her father since she left home at 16.'

'When are you seeing her again?'

'Next Monday. She's due to come into hospital on Friday for surgery the following Monday. They need to do some investigations and they want her to settle down a bit before they operate.'

'What's going to happen to the children?'

'We're trying to sort it out,' said Sarah. 'It looks as though they'll have to go into care.'

'The 13 year old's not going to take kindly to that, is she?' said Chris.

'I know,' said Sarah. 'That's one of the things I wanted to ask you. I'm not sure I can handle a bolshie adolescent.'

'Have you spoken to the GP yet?' asked Chris. 'How does he feel about it?'

'He feels a bit out of his depth,' said Sarah. 'He's going to ask you to see her.'

'That's fine,' said Chris, 'I see quite a few adolescents these days.'

Sarah heaved a sigh of relief, 'That'll be great. Thanks.'

'It sounds as though you're doing fine with this lady, Sarah. What about *you*. What's it doing to you?'

'Damn. I knew you'd ask that. I'm all right.' Sarah's voice was tense.

'Are you?' Chris was very gentle now.

Suddenly, the tears came and Sarah groped for her handkerchief. 'I'm sorry,' she gulped. 'I'm sorry to be so stupid. It's just that I'm dreadfully tired and, and . . .' Chris and Caroline sat silently. 'It's just . . . it's just that Katie's 29 and so am I and my two children are more or less the same age as her younger ones . . .'

'So you identify with her?'

'Oh, Chris. It's horrible. It's like looking in a mirror – but it's one of those distorting mirrors. I feel so guilty. I've got Gordon and my kids are so lovely – and Katie's got nothing. And now on top of it all, she's got cancer. It's just not fair.'

'Sarah,' said Chris quietly, 'life isn't fair, is it? But it's up to us

19

to try and redress the balance. Katie isn't alone now. She's got you but you won't be any use to her if you get things out of proportion.'

'I know,' said Sarah, blowing her nose hard. 'I'm sorry. I'm being stupid.'

'No,' Chris was quick to answer. 'You're not being stupid. You're just human and vulnerable and that's good. But you have to learn to live with your vulnerability, to use it to increase your powers of empathy, but not let yourself be destroyed. Do you understand what I am saying?'

Sarah nodded, 'Yes,' she said. 'I do. Thanks.'

'That's fine,' said Chris. 'But over the next couple of weeks I want you to think again about the issue of professional distance that we talked about . . .'

'I know,' Sarah interrupted him, 'and to get it into my thick head that Katie is a *client*, not my best friend . . .'

'That's it,' said Chris. 'Once you're clear about that, you'll be able to be even more available to her. Are you all right now?'

'Sure. I'm fine. Let's listen to Caroline.'

'Phew,' said Caroline, who had been listening intently to Sarah's discussion with the psychiatrist. 'Thank God my lady's not quite as complicated as yours. I told you about her two weeks ago: she's 40 and she's got breast cancer. I met her on her first visit to the GP, right after he'd told her she'd have to see the surgeon.'

'Oh yes. I remember,' said Chris, 'she's the lady who thought her husband would leave her if she had a mastectomy.'

'That's right. Well, she saw the surgeon last week and now she's in a real state.'

'How come?' asked Chris.

'Well, it was a particularly busy Clinic and she had to wait for ages, so by the time she went in to see Mr Dalton she was really anxious.'

'And?'

'Well – you know how Mr Dalton is. He's a wonderful surgeon, but communication isn't really his forte. Anyway, according to Mary, when he'd finished examining her he said in a brisk voice: "Well, my dear. You'll be better off without that." He was lucky she didn't freak out completely. As it was, she sat there, practically starkers and burst into tears all over him, whereupon the great man says, "Now, now, Mrs Carlisle, we don't want any of that do we?" '

'Oh my Lord,' said Chris. 'What did she do then?'

'She just sobbed the more and he walked out and left the nurse to pick up the pieces. When I saw John, the husband, he was all for changing surgeons, going private, going to London, anything so long as his wife never laid eyes on Tim Dalton again.'

'Oh God.' The psychiatrist raised his eyes to heaven. 'When will these guys learn they're dealing with frightened women, not a herd of cows.'

'Oh, come off it, Chris!' Sarah's voice was sharp. 'Mr Dalton's not that bad. He just doesn't understand how fragile some people are. He really cares about his patients.'

'It's all very well for you to defend him, Sarah,' Caroline was angry now. 'But it really isn't good enough. Mary's traumatized enough without being exposed to an insensitive boor like Tim Dalton.'

'Okay girls. Let's get on with it. How is she now, Caroline?'

'Fragile, to put it mildly,' said Caroline. 'Her husband's determined to change surgeons so Michael has arranged for her to see Mr Giles at his private clinic tomorrow.'

It was Chris's turn to be angry: 'It makes me so ashamed of the profession to think that this couple has to fork out money they can ill afford just for someone to treat them like human beings.'

'Poor old Tim,' Sarah returned to the surgeon's defence. 'Most of his patients worship the ground he walks on. Anyway, he must be due to retire soon. He's one of the last of the dinosaurs. Most of the younger surgeons are very good with women with breast cancer. She'll be fine with Tony Giles, he's a real sweetie. His wife had breast cancer, so he has a lot of insight into how his patients feel.'

'Right,' said Chris. 'So, how's all this left you feeling, Caroline?'

'Okay, but I'm worried about Mary. It isn't really my job to do long term support with our patients. I haven't got the time. But she's clearly going to need a lot of help in coming to terms with losing a breast and, without being too gloomy, my guess is she's not curable and she'll be in trouble with recurrence before too long.'

'How would it be if she came up to the Cancer Support

Centre?' said Sarah. 'If she and her husband come up we can see them both and assess what help they need.'

'That'd be great, Sarah. Thanks. Do they need a referral letter?'

'It would help if we had some details, but it's not essential. The whole idea is that it's a drop in centre and people can self-refer.'

'How long's that been going Sarah?' asked Chris. It sounds like really good news.'

'It's very new – we've been open about two months – the numbers are just starting to build up.'

'Who's involved with it?' asked Caroline.

'There's a group of us – we call ourselves the Cancer Support Team. There's me and Clare, the oncology support nurse, Jackie the co-ordinator and a group of volunteers.'

'What about medical back up?' asked Chris.

'Oh, the oncologists are pretty supportive, and Dr Callaghan the palliative care specialist is being paid a session a week to supervise and support.'

'Sounds wonderful. But don't overdo it, Sarah. You've got to look after yourself. Learn to guard your boundaries. Are you listening?'

Sarah grinned. 'Thanks Chris. I do try, I do.'

'Right then. Are we done?' Chris looked up at the two women.

'I think so.' Caroline paused. 'Except – could I see you on your own for a few minutes, Chris? There's something I'm really worried about.'

'I'm off anyway.' Sarah jumped up and started gathering her things together. 'Gordon's getting supper tonight and he'll be cross if I'm late.'

'You've got him well trained, Sarah,' said Caroline wistfully, 'Geoff can hardly boil an egg!'

When Sarah had gone, Chris and Caroline sat down again. 'Well Caroline. What's up?' said Chris gently. 'Are you getting low again?'

'No. I'm fine. The surgery job suits me just fine. No. It's about Michael. We're really worried about him, and as you know him I thought I could talk to you.'

'What's the trouble?' Chris was wary. Informal 'referrals' were often fraught with problems.

'Well,' said Caroline, 'he's been really irritable and preoccupied lately, quite sharp sometimes. And then a couple of weeks ago Molly the receptionist went in to take him his coffee and he'd been crying.'

'That doesn't sound like Michael.' Chris was worried now. 'Have you any idea what's up?'

'Well, Molly's got a hunch that it's to do with Jane, his wife. Molly thinks their marriage is in trouble.'

'What makes her think that?' asked Chris quietly.

'She says it's just a hunch,' said Caroline, 'but Molly's pretty shrewd and she adores Michael. I'd trust her judgement.'

Chris sighed, 'What do you want me to do?'

'I don't know, Chris. It's just that I'm sure he needs help and I thought, well, I thought you'd know what to do.'

'But Caroline,' Chris was mildly exasperated; 'I can't just ring Michael up and ask him how his marriage is – now can I?'

'Oh you'll think of something, Chris,' said Caroline grinning. 'I know you will.'

'All right. I'll have a think, but I'm not promising anything.'

Caroline grinned at him. 'You're an angel Chris, thanks so much. Michael's such a lovely man. I can't bear to think of him in trouble. Now,' she said, as she gathered her things together, 'I must think about what to give Geoff and the kids for supper.'

5

Jane Howard sighed – a long low sigh, and then, feeling the tears begin again, laid her head on her arms and gave herself up to despair. After a while the tears stopped and she felt strong enough to make a cup of coffee. I just don't know what's wrong with me, she thought. Why do I feel like this? What's wrong with Mike? Why doesn't he seem to love me anymore? Why doesn't he spend more time with us? Perhaps he's bored with me, got someone else. Oh God . . .

Slowly, Jane drank her coffee and tried to pull herself together. It was nine o'clock. Six hours before she had to pick up the children from school. What should she do? What *was* there to do? If only I could sleep, she thought desperately. If only I wasn't so tired. If only I could concentrate; read a book; make Sally a dress. Anything. Perhaps I could go and have coffee with Fanny. That's it. She'll cheer me up. Jane heaved herself out of her chair and went to look up Fanny's phone number. She dialled the number and waited, but as she heard the phone ring she was besieged again by self doubt. Oh God, she thought, What's the point? She won't want to see me like this. I'm not fit company for anyone.

Fanny's voice answered, bright and in control as always. 'Hello?' she said. Jane stood there numb, and then putting the phone down began to weep once more. Oh. Damn. Damn. Damn. What the hell's wrong with me? I'm just so tired, so tired. I need to sleep. I just need to sleep. Jane sat at the kitchen table again, the tears falling unheeded into her coffee as she tried to think clearly. I've got six hours before the kids come home she calculated. Six hours. Perhaps I could sleep now. At least I could try. Perhaps I could take something – it'd have worn off in a few hours.

Searching through the top drawer of Michael's desk, she found a medical sample of sleeping pills and, taking all three, took herself off to bed.

It was around four-thirty in the afternoon when the phone rang on Michael's desk. He picked it up irritably, 'What is it?' he said sharply, 'I'm with a patient.'

Molly stood her ground. 'I'm sorry Dr Howard, but it's your children's school and they say it's urgent.'

Michael's heart missed a beat. The children, he thought. There must have been an accident. O Lord. 'Put them through Molly.'

'Dr Howard?' The headmistress's voice was apologetic. Doctors are such busy people. 'I'm sorry to bother you, but . . .'

'Yes, Mrs Thompson,' said Michael anxiously, 'what is it?'

'Oh, it's nothing serious,' she said, trying not to alarm him. 'It's just that Mrs Howard hasn't come to pick up the children and I don't quite know what to do.'

Relief turned instantly to anger. What the hell's Jane playing at? he thought. God knows she's got little enough to do all day. Picking up the kids is her responsibility. Pulling himself together he asked coldly, 'Have you tried telephoning her? Perhaps she's been delayed.'

Mrs Thompson struggled to control herself. What an arrogant man, did he think she was half witted? 'Dr Howard,' she said firmly, 'I've been trying to contact your wife for the last three quarters of an hour, but the telephone's engaged. I don't know what else you'd like me to do.'

'Engaged?' Michael's anger turned to anxiety once more. 'All this time. Are you sure?'

'Yes, Dr Howard. *Quite* sure. Now, could you please arrange to have Sally and Andrew picked up as soon as possible. They're tired and hungry and I'm afraid I have to leave very soon.'

Michael knew the voice of authority when he heard it. 'Of course, Mrs Thompson. I'll get someone down to the school right away.'

'Thank you, doctor. We'll be waiting for you.'

Waiting for *me*? echoed Michael silently to himself. Stupid woman. Does she think I can just walk out of the surgery to pick up my kids from school? Michael looked at the woman sitting patiently beside his desk. 'I'm sorry Mrs Smith,' he said. 'There's something I have to sort out. I'll be with you in just a minute.' He rose swiftly and walked out of the room. 'Molly!' he called as he strode along. Molly Gibson left the reception desk and walked down the corridor to meet him.

'Yes doctor?' said his unflappable receptionist.

'Molly,' said Michael, 'Jane hasn't turned up to collect the kids and the school's getting edgy. Have you got someone who could go and pick them up for me. Better bring them here and I'll take them home after surgery.'

'What's happened to Jane, doctor?' said Molly, sensing his agitation.

'How the hell should I know Molly,' said Michael tersely. 'They've tried to ring her and the phone's engaged.'

'I hope nothing's wrong, doctor,' said Molly, a touch gloomily.

Michael could not bear to hear his own dark thoughts reflected. 'Don't be stupid, Molly. What could be wrong? Just be a dear and sort this out for me. I must go back to Mrs Smith and her piles.'

It was nearly eight by the time Michael and the children arrived home and the house was in darkness. Michael's heart gave a little lurch and he felt a wave of nausea sweep over him. Where was Jane? Surely she couldn't just have walked out?

'Where's Mummy, Daddy?' Andrew asked for the umpteenth time. 'Is she ill?'

'I don't *know* Andrew,' said Michael, trying to keep the anxiety out of his voice. 'I'm sure she's fine. Something important must have delayed her.' He opened the door and turned on the hall lights. 'Now, Sally, will you and Andrew please go up to your rooms and get changed while I get some supper.'

While the children went slowly up the stairs, Michael went into the kitchen. There on the table were the breakfast dishes and an empty coffee mug. No note, he thought. Thank God. Where the hell is she? He went through the utility room into the garage: Jane's car was in its place. How bizarre.

'Daddy! Daddy. Mummy's asleep in bed!' Sally's voice was shrill.

Asleep, he thought, at this time of day? Michael bounded up the stairs two at a time and went into the bedroom. Sure enough, there was Jane, fast asleep with a bottle of whisky and an empty glass beside her bed. Whisky? he thought incredulously. But Jane doesn't drink whisky.

'Sally! Andrew!' he said firmly to the children at his heels, 'will you please go to your rooms. Mummy isn't well.'

Alone with Jane, Michael knelt down beside the bed and gently touched her face. Jane gave a little moan but didn't wake. 'Jane darling,' said her husband. 'Wake up. Wake up.'

Slowly Jane opened her eyes and struggled to sit up. 'Michael? What's happened. What time is it?'

'It's eight o'clock, Jane,' said Michael, rising from his knees to sit beside her. 'When did you go to bed?'

'I don't know, Mike,' she said. 'This morning sometime. I was so tired. I took three sleeping pills and then I thought if I had some whisky too I'd be sure to sleep.'

'But darling,' asked her husband, 'whatever possessed you to take sleeping pills in the middle of the morning? No wonder you've slept all day.'

'Oh Mike,' Jane began to cry. 'I felt so awful. I was so sad I just couldn't bear it. I just wanted to blot out the pain for a few hours.'

'What pain?' Michael's voice was anxious. You didn't tell me you had a pain.'

'Not *that* sort of pain. It's a sort of pain in my heart. I feel grey, empty. All the world is grey. I feel hollow, as though there's nothing left worth living for.'

Michael put his arms around his wife and held her close. 'Jane, my darling, why didn't you tell me? Why did you keep it all to yourself?'

Jane buried her face against her husband's chest. 'You're always so busy Michael, she said. 'I didn't want to bother you. I didn't think . . . I didn't think . . .' The words stuck in Jane's throat and all that came out was a muffled sob.

Michael held her tighter and smoothed her hair like a child's. 'What are you trying to say Jane? Tell me?'

'Oh Mike – I didn't think you cared.'

Now it was Michael's turn to cry and they clung to each other like desperate children and wept.

'Daddy . . .' a plaintive voice sounded from behind the door. 'We're hungry. When are we going to have supper?'

'Oh, my God. The children.' Gently, Michael laid his wife back on her pillow and pulling himself together called out. 'I'll be down in a minute, Sal. Get the eggs and the bacon out of the fridge and lay the table. We're having scrambled eggs and bacon. And, Sally, could you lay a tray for Mummy, please. She's not very well and I'm going to bring her supper in bed.

Later that evening, when they had all had supper and the children had gone to bed, Michael and Jane sat together in their bedroom. 'Jane,' said Michael. 'This sadness, this grey, hollow feeling: how long have you had it?'

'I don't know Mike,' said his wife. 'It's sort of crept up on me. I've been sleeping badly for a couple of months . . .'

'But you didn't tell me?' said Mike, perplexed.

'Mike,' said Jane quietly, 'you didn't ask. You used to ask me how I was, how my day had been, once, but lately . . . you've been so busy.'

'Jane darling,' Michael was appalled. 'I'm *so* sorry,' he said. 'I've been so preoccupied that I didn't notice. Or rather, I thought you'd stopped caring about *me*. I even thought . . .'

'What, Mike?'

'I thought you'd got someone else.'

Jane began to cry again. 'Oh Michael, how *could* you. As if I would. As if anyone would want me, the way I am now!'

'What do you mean?' said her husband. 'The way you are now?'

'Well, look at me. I'm a mess,' she said. 'I've lost my figure. My hair's awful. I'm just a boring housewife. No one would look at me.'

'Jane, Jane.' Michael felt sick with grief and shame. 'You're my wife. I love you. And you're not a mess.' Jane began to cry again and he held her tight.

Next morning, Michael arranged with his senior partner for one of their colleagues to do his morning surgery and asked a friend to take the children to school. Then, taking two mugs of coffee upstairs, he sat down on the bed beside his wife. 'Jane,' he said gently.

'Yes.' Her voice was weak – she was still close to tears.

'Jane, darling. I've spoken to Bill Shaw and he's coming out to see you after surgery.'

'Oh Mike,' she begged. 'I don't want to see anyone. I'll be all right.'

'Sweetheart, you're not well and I don't think I should treat you. I'm too close to you and I can't see things straight.'

Bill Shaw, Michael's senior partner, was a kindly man of 60 odd. He showed the anxious Michael out of the room and sat down by Jane's bed.

'Well Jane,' he said quietly, 'What's been happening to you?'

'I don't know, Bill,' her voice faltered. 'It's come on over the past few months. I can't seem to sleep properly, or rather I wake up in the middle of the night and can't get back to sleep again. And I just feel so low and useless.'

'Do you find yourself weeping?' Bill asked.

'Oh God. I can't seem to stop. I just feel so sad, although I don't really know what I've got to be sad about. I'm so lucky really. I've got a good husband, two lovely children, everything to live for, and yet . . . everything seems so pointless.'

'Pointless?'

'Yes,' she said. 'Sometimes . . . I feel that life just isn't worth living.'

'Jane, I want you to answer me truthfully. Have you ever thought of ending your life?' There was a long pause. Bill waited quietly for Jane to speak.

'Yes,' her reply shook him. 'Often. I think about it most days.'

'Have you ever thought about how you'd do it?' he asked quietly.

'I thought pills would be easiest or perhaps the car.'

'Oh Jane. Why didn't you come and see me? Why didn't you ask for help?'

'I don't know. I suppose I thought there was nothing anyone could do. I've felt so worthless. I didn't think anyone would want to bother with me.'

'Jane, my dear. I'd like to go and have a chat with Michael now and then we'll be back. Try to rest a little.' He left the room quietly and went downstairs.

'Michael, your wife is seriously depressed. Had you not noticed?'

Michael hung his head feeling like a fifth year medical student. 'I noticed she was behaving differently towards me, but no, I didn't realise she was depressed until last night.'

Bill looked at his young partner and had difficulty controlling his anger. He thought, how the hell could you not have noticed? But he bit his lip and said nothing.

'What are you going to do?' said Michael. 'Do you think she needs antidepressants?'

'Of course she needs antidepressants.' Bill was short now. 'She's suicidal. Didn't she tell you?'

Michael gulped. 'Suicidal? Surely not.'

'Michael – she's just told me. She thinks about it every day.'

'Oh my God.' Michael put his head in his hands and began to cry.

Bill cursed himself silently. Poor bugger, he thought. I was too hard on him. God knows I'm not that good a husband myself. We, none of us are. We spend all we've got on our work and take our wives and kids for granted. 'I'm sorry, Mike. I didn't mean to be sharp. I'm just worried about her. I think she's at risk and we may need to get her into hospital. Which of the psychiatrists would you like to see her?'

Michael was very sober now. 'Chris,' he said. 'Chris Walker. He's the one I know best.'

'Right. Have you got his number? I'll ring him now.'

Slowly, the two doctors went up the stairs, and Jane looked up as they entered. Michael sat on the edge of the bed and took his wife's hand.

'Jane . . .' Bill's voice was extra kind. 'Michael and I have been discussing how best we can help you. We think that you have a depressive illness and that you need some antidepressants. I've taken the liberty of asking Chris Walker to come out and see you. Is that all right?'

Jane's eyes widened with fear 'I don't want to see a psychiatrist,' she said. 'I'm not mad. I'm just tired.' She was near to tears.

Michael tightened his grip on her hand. 'My dearest one,' he said, 'of *course* you're not mad: but you *are* very depressed and I've been a fool not to have noticed it. Chris will tell us what the best treatment is for you. Please see him. Please – for my sake.'

Once again the tears coursed down Jane's face and she buried her head in the pillow muttering, 'Oh, if I must. But I don't *want* to.'

Michael stroked his wife's hair gently as Bill rose to his feet. 'I think you'd better take the rest of today off, Michael,' he said. 'Get Chris to give me a ring when he's seen Jane.'

30

Michael nodded. 'Thanks Bill,' he said. 'I can't tell you how grateful I am. I'm sorry I've been so stupid.'

Bill let his hand rest briefly on Michael's shoulder. 'We live and learn, Mike,' he said. 'We live and learn.'

It was half past one when a very dejected Michael opened the door to Chris. The psychiatrist looked at him thoughtfully. 'Hello Mike,' he said. 'Sorry I'm late. It's been a long morning.'

Michael's relief was evident. 'Thanks Chris,' he said. 'I'm really grateful to you for coming. Have you had lunch? I'm just having mine.'

'I could use a coffee' said Chris, 'and some bread and cheese if you've got it. I don't usually have time for lunch. This is a luxury.'

The two men ate quietly together at the kitchen table. When he'd finished eating, Chris picked up his coffee and said quietly, 'What's happening, Mike?'

'Jane's depressed,' said Michael, immediately on his guard now that Chris was in professional mode. 'She took some sleeping pills yesterday morning, took the phone off the hook and slept right through till the evening. The school had to ring me to pick up the kids. She was still asleep when we got home, flat out with a bottle of whisky by the bed. The kids found her.'

Chris was grave. 'How many pills did she take?'

'Oh, only three, thank God. She found a sample in my desk.'

'And how long has she been unwell?'

'The awful thing is . . .' said Michael, 'I hadn't noticed she was depressed. My own wife . . . severely depressed, and I just didn't notice.' Michael's voice began to crack and his eyes filled with tears.

Chris sat quietly while Michael struggled to find his handkerchief and blew his nose, then got up. 'Look Mike. I've only got three quarters of an hour at the moment. How would it be if I saw Jane now and then you and I can talk at length this evening.'

'Thanks, Chris,' said Michael gratefully. 'That would be very good.'

Half an hour later, Chris came back into the kitchen and put his hand gently on Michael's shoulder as he sat slumped over the kitchen table. 'She'll be okay, Mike, with some medication and a lot of support. Can you take a week off work to look after her?

If you can't I think I'd better take her into the Elms for a few days.'

Michael was suddenly appalled at the thought of his wife in a psychiatric ward. 'No, no,' he said, 'don't take her away. I'll take some leave. Bill said he'd get a locum if I needed some time off.'

'That's fine. Now, here's a prescription. Try to get her started on it today. It'll be good if you can be around for a few days to give Jane the support she needs.'

'What about the suicide talk, Chris – do you think she's really at risk?'

'I think the risk is much less now that you two are communicating again. She was convinced you didn't love her and that was her principle reason for thinking that life wasn't worth living.'

Michael's eyes filled with tears again.

'Tonight, Mike,' he said. 'I'll be back around six-thirty. We'll talk then, okay?' Michael wiped his tears and stood up. 'Thanks, Chris. Tonight then.'

6

It was just after three when Chris got back to his office. 'Any phone calls?' he asked the middle-aged woman working at a word processor.

His secretary, Karen Innes, smiled. 'You're lucky,' she said; 'only one, and that was a drug rep. You've a patient for three o'clock, but she's not here yet.'

'She may not turn up,' said Chris, but as he spoke the clinic door slammed and there was the sound of footsteps on the stairs. 'Hello,' he said cheerfully. 'You must be Emma. I'm Dr Walker. Could you take a seat for a moment and I'll be right with you.'

For once, Emma was lost for words. She hadn't expected the doctor to be nice to her, and she certainly hadn't expected him to be good looking. Not knowing quite what to say, she sat down as she was bidden and looked around her. This wasn't bad for a hospital. There was carpet on the floor and the furniture was modern. Emma wasn't quite sure what she'd expected. Loonies in the corridor? The doctor old and crabby with steel rimmed glasses? Bars on the window?

Her musing was interrupted by the doctor's voice. 'Right, Emma. I'm sorry to keep you waiting. Would you like some coffee?'

'Oh.' Emma was startled. 'Yes, please.'

'Milk? Sugar?'

'Milk please. No sugar.' Emma sat, momentarily baffled, trying to take stock of her unaccustomed surroundings. She still had not sussed things out when the doctor returned with two mugs of coffee and handed her one.

'Right,' he said. 'Here you are. I'm glad you've come.'

'Glad?' Emma was surprised. 'Glad? Why?'

'Well,' said Chris. 'I thought perhaps you mightn't. That you might not want to.'

'I came because I promised Mum, and I knew she'd go on at me if I didn't. But I still don't understand *why*. There's nothing wrong with *me*.'

33

'No one's saying there is anything *wrong* with you Emma,' said Chris firmly. 'We just thought you might find it helpful to talk to someone.'

'Why? Why would I want to talk to *you*?'

'Well, Emma . . .' Chris grinned at her, 'most people need someone to talk to – and I'm quite a good listener.'

'No one wants to listen to *me*.' Emma was angry now. 'No one wants to listen to kids. They don't count.'

'What about your mum, Emma?' said Chris, 'Doesn't she listen?'

'Not really. She's always going on at me. Tidy up your room, Emma. Help me get the tea, Emma. Mind you're back by ten, Emma.'

'And are you back by ten?'

'Not me,' said Emma cockily. 'That's when things are just getting going. That's when I come alive.'

'So, you're a night person, are you?'

'Yes. That's me. I hate going to bed early – you miss all the fun.'

'What do you do at night then?' asked Chris casually.

Emma was guarded now. 'Oh, all sorts,' she said. 'Have fun. Hang around with my friends.'

'Have you got a boyfriend, Emma?' Chris' voice was softer now.

Emma smirked a little. 'Yes' she said. 'Sure.'

'What's his name?' asked Chris.

'What's that to you?' said Emma suspiciously.

'It's okay.' said Chris. 'You don't have to tell me. I just wondered.'

Emma relaxed. 'Oh, well,' she said, 'his name's Joe.'

'And are you fond of him?'

'Yes. I suppose I am.'

'How old's Joe? Does he go to school with you?'

'He's 16,' said Emma, 'and he's two classes above me.'

'Do you mind if I ask you something a bit more personal, Emma?' said Chris.

Emma was on her guard again, but flattered to be treated like an adult. 'Depends what it is,' she said.

'Do you go to bed with Joe?'

34

For a minute the girl was puzzled, then she said, 'Have sex with him, you mean? Of course I do.'

'Of course?' questioned Chris gently.

'Well, everyone does. All my crowd have sex with their friends.' She was defensive now. 'It's natural, isn't it?'

'Well,' said Chris thoughtfully, 'I suppose it depends a bit on the culture one grows up in. Some people would think you're a bit young to be having sex.'

'I'm nearly 14,' said Emma. 'I can handle it.'

'Can you, Emma? Can you?' said Chris, looking her straight in the eye.

Emma bit her lip. 'Sure,' she said, but her bravado was wearing thin.

'You're pretty young, you know Emma,' said Chris. 'Your body's not yet fully developed at 13. You might hurt yourself.'

For a moment, Emma was silent, then she burst out angrily, 'Well, why did Dad make me do it then?'

So. I was right thought Chris angrily as Emma confirmed his hunch. 'Your Dad, Emma?' he said. 'When was that?'

'When I was little, about four or five. I used to stay with him at weekends.'

Bastard! thought Chris, as he asked her, 'And how do you feel about that now, Emma?'

'I hated it.' Emma was crying now; the perky teenager had vanished, leaving a desolate child. A little girl betrayed by her father, estranged from her mother − a very lonely little girl.

'Did you tell your mum about it? Does she know?'

'I tried to, a few years ago, when I was about ten, but she belted me and said I was a filthy little liar.'

Chris was quiet while Emma dried her eyes on the health service tissues he handed her. Then he spoke, 'What do you want to do about it, Emma?'

'Do about it? What can I do?' she said desperately. 'He's my dad, isn't he? I don't want to get him into trouble.'

Suddenly, Emma's inner child took charge and she began to sob uncontrollably. 'I'm so miserable,' she said. 'I don't know what to do. I hate sex. It makes me feel dirty but I'm afraid Joe'll leave me if I won't do it with him. What can I do?'

'This is where I come in Emma,' said Chris quietly. 'You see,

35

you're under 16 and Joe is breaking the law by what he does with you. I think you need to be protected from him and from yourself for a while.'

'What are you going to do? Will they take me into care?' Emma was really frightened now.

'No. There's no need for that, but I'd like you to see a lady called Cathy who will talk to you about the way you feel and help you to understand things a bit better.'

Emma still looked anxious and Chris smiled. 'Is that all right?' he said. The girl nodded.

'Now, Emma,' Chris said, 'I need to talk to you about your mum. She really needs you at the moment.'

'You mean because she's sick?'

'Yes. That's what I mean. Has she told you about it?'

Emma was subdued. 'She tried to, the other night, but, I was going out – and I didn't listen very carefully.'

'What did she tell you, Emma?'

Emma seemed uncertain. 'She said she had cancer of the cervix but I didn't really understand what she was on about.'

'Do you know what the cervix is?' said Chris.

Emma looked doubtful. Damn that school. How can she be so worldly wise and yet so ignorant? 'Let me get a bit of paper,' he said, 'and I'll draw you a picture.'

Emma could sense his discomfort and grinned sheepishly. 'Sorry,' she said, 'but I played truant when we did biology at school.'

'It's all right,' said Chris. 'Look, this is the uterus, where a baby grows, and this is the vagina. Are you with me?' Emma nodded. 'Right. Now the bottom of the uterus, the bit which is at the top of the vagina, is called the neck of the uterus, or the cervix. Now this part can become cancerous, and that's what's happened to your mum.'

Emma was scared now. 'Will she, will she be all right?' she said. 'They can treat it, can't they?'

'Yes,' said Chris, thankful he'd had his conversation with Sarah. 'She's lucky, they've caught it early. But she's going to have to have a big operation and it'll take her a long time to get back to normal.'

'What about the kids?' said Emma. 'Who'll look after the baby?'

'I don't know, Emma. Your mum's got to work that out with the social worker.'

'I'll help,' she said. Suddenly, there was a different Emma sitting there. The pert teenager and the frightened child had been replaced by a determined, 13 year old. 'I can cook. I'll help.'

'Well done, Emma,' said Chris smiling. 'Your mum needs a lot of support right now. She really needs you.'

'I know. I'd better be going home.' She stood up decisively. Chris stood up too. 'Are you going out tonight?' he asked.

Emma looked him straight in the eye. 'No,' she said. 'I'm going to stay in with Mum.'

'Good girl. Now, Emma, one more thing: I'd like to meet your mum. Do you think I could come and see her tomorrow, or would you and she like to come and see me here?'

'I'll bring her here,' said Emma firmly. 'What time?'

Chris hesitated: 'How about four o'clock?'

'That's fine. I get off school at half three.'

Chris made a note in his diary. 'Four o'clock it is,' he said. 'Goodbye, Emma. I'll see you tomorrow.'

Chris accompanied Emma to the door and grinned at the cheery wave she gave him as she walked across the car park. Back upstairs he went in to his secretary. 'Have I got anyone for four o'clock tomorrow, Karen?'

Karen looked in the big appointments diary. 'Mr Adamson,' she said.

'Oh, blast. I forgot. Could you ring him, please, Karen, and ask him to come at another time. Tell him I'm really sorry, but it's an emergency.'

Karen, pencil in hand looked up at him calmly. 'And what shall I put for tomorrow at four?' she said.

'Oh, Roberts, Karen. A Mrs Katie Roberts and her daughter Emma.' Karen wrote the names in her book. 'Would you like a coffee?' she said. 'Karen,' said Chris. 'You're an angel. I'll be in my office.'

7

It was gone six by the time Chris pulled up outside the Howards' house. Michael was waiting for him and answered the door at once and led him through into the kitchen, where Sally and Andrew were devouring huge helpings of beans and sausages.

'Come and say hello to the kids for a minute. I've told them you're looking after Mummy.'

The children looked up from their supper, though Andrew was clearly more interested in his food than in Chris.

'Hello, Sally,' said Chris. 'How are you?'

'I'm fine thanks. Will Mummy be all right, Uncle Chris?' she asked anxiously. 'Will you make her well again?'

Chris smiled. 'I'm sure she'll be just fine, Sally, but it'll take a little while. You and Andrew will have to try extra hard to be helpful for the next few weeks.'

'I'm going to feed the cat,' said Andrew proudly, losing a few baked beans from an overful mouth.

'That's very good, Andrew. Well done,' said Chris smiling.

Michael stood up. 'Now children,' he said, 'when you've finished your supper I want you to clear the table and put the plates in the dishwasher. Then you can go and watch the television. Uncle Chris and I are going to have a talk in my study. Sally, if the phone goes, could you take a message please, and tell them I'll ring back. Okay?'

Sally nodded solemnly and smiled up at her father as he patted her shoulder on his way to the door.

'How's Jane?' said Chris as he sipped his coffee.'

'Better thanks,' said Michael. 'She's slept quite a bit. I had a nap with her this afternoon and we had a bit of a cuddle'.

Chris paused and then asked quietly, 'How long is it since you and Jane made love, Mike?'

Michael gulped. He hadn't expected this. He looked down at his hands and said slowly, 'It's been a while. Three or four months, I suppose.'

'Why's that?'

'I don't know really. Jane's been so tired and, and . . . To tell you the truth, I just haven't felt like it. And . . .'

'Yes?'

'I've been sleeping in the spare room for the past six weeks or so. You see, I've been sleeping so badly, I didn't want to disturb Jane.'

'Is that the only reason?'

'No, damn you. I didn't feel like sharing a bed. I wanted to be alone.'

'What's wrong, Mike?' said Chris, 'What's at the bottom of it all? Is there someone else?'

Michael began to cry: harsh desperate sobs that seemed to come from the depths of his belly. Chris waited, saying nothing. After a while Michael spoke, slowly and painfully. 'There was, very briefly,' he said. 'It's over now. Jane doesn't know and I don't want her to know . . . Oh Chris, I'm so ashamed.'

Chris' voice was very gentle: 'Would it help to talk about it?'

Michael was thoughtful, then, taking a deep breath said, 'Yes. If you don't mind. They say confession is good for the soul. God knows I need forgiveness and I've no one else to ask.'

Chris waited, while Michael gathered his thoughts. 'It happened two months ago. I was away on a course, a psycho sexual counselling course, believe it or not. We did a lot of work in pairs, role play, you understand and very open discussion. I was paired up with a young GP trainee, a stunning blonde of about 26. Anyway, we worked really well together: I've never talked so openly to anyone about myself or about sex. It was wonderful – an amazing experience. That night, after the course dinner, we had a couple of whiskies together and then she said, 'How about a bit of practical work.' She handed me a scrap of paper with her room number on it, and then said good night, and she was gone.'

'And you accepted her offer?' said Chris, taking care not to betray his feelings.

'Yes, I did. Not right away, though. I sat there and had an orange juice and thought about it. At first I thought no, it would be wrong. And then, I thought, well, who'd ever know? We were miles from home. There was no one who really knew me. Somehow, I convinced myself that this was time out, that I was entitled to a little fling, a bit of fun – so, I said good night to the others and went up and knocked on her door.'

'And was it fun?'

'Oh God, Chris,' said Michael, 'it was amazing. I've never had sex like it! I don't know where she learned her stuff.'

Chris grinned. 'Maybe they do special courses in Medical School these days!' There was a pause while both men regained their concentration.

'How did you feel afterwards, Mike? Did you arrange to see her again?'

'I wanted to. God knows I wanted to, but she said no.'

'And that was that?'

'In one sense yes, but in another, no.'

'How do you mean?' said Chris.

'I've carried the memory of that night around with me day and night for weeks. I can't stop thinking about it. I can remember it *so* clearly: the feel of her, her perfume, the colour of her hair, and, and the way she made me feel. Oh God, Chris. I might just as well be having a torrid affair for all the attention I've paid to Jane.' Michael looked down at his shoes and his eyes filled with tears yet again.

Chris waited, quietly attentive. Michael looked up at him. 'I've been a bastard,' he said, 'haven't I?'

Chris sighed. 'You've been weak,' he said, 'and selfish. That's for sure. But it happens to a lot of good people. You're not alone.'

'What should I do, Chris? Should I tell Jane?'

'Why would you want to do that?' said Chris quietly.

'To ask her forgiveness, I suppose,' said Michael.

'So that you can feel clean again?'

Michael nodded, suddenly sensing the other's anger.

'And what will that do to her?' asked Chris.

'I hadn't thought about that.' Michael was barely audible.

'Well, think about it now,' said Chris. 'Think hard.'

Michael's eyes lowered. 'It'll hurt her terribly. It'll confirm her fears that I don't love her any more.'

'Right! And do you love her?'

'Yes. I do. I love her very much indeed.' Michael spoke slowly and quietly.

'So – what would be best for Jane?'

40

'Not to tell her.'

'Are you sure?' said Chris.

'Yes. Unless she were to find out.'

'Is that likely?'

'No. There's no way that Nicky would tell her. She's not that sort of woman,' said Michael.

'Right,' said Chris. 'Then I suggest you say nothing. The guilt is yours. Live with it and learn from it.'

'I could have lost my wife and kids.' There was self pity in his voice now.

'You could.'

'Oh God, how could I be so stupid?'

'Because you're human,' said Chris gently. 'Because you're a man. And because you're no better than the rest of us at looking after yourself and your family.'

'What do you mean?' asked Michael, hoping perhaps that Chris would make him feel less bad by revealing some indiscretion of his own.

Chris, however, was not in the mood for sharing secrets. 'Let's talk about your lifestyle, Mike,' he said firmly, 'your family, your marriage. What time do you leave home in the morning?'

'Around eight. I like to get to the surgery early to do a bit of reading.'

'And Jane? What's she doing?'

'Getting the kids to school,' said Michael, surprised that Chris should ask such an obvious question.

'And what time do you get home?'

'Oh, eight,' he said, 'sometimes nine.'

'What are you doing till then?'

'Surgery visits. Dictating. Sometimes I go to the medical centre and have a drink. It's useful to get to know the consultants.'

'And what's Jane doing?' Chris was at pains to keep his tone neutral.

'Feeding the kids. Putting them to bed.'

'What does Jane do when the kids are at school?'

'I don't really know. Housework, shopping. Whatever.'

'Have you ever asked her what she does?' said Chris.

Incredibly, Michael was still unaware of where Chris was leading him. 'No, not really.'

41

'What did Jane do before you married her?' asked the psychiatrist.

'She was a nurse. She was senior staff nurse on the oncology ward, at the Royal Vic.'

'And does she miss it?'

'Well, yes. But I, we thought it was important that she should be at home while the kids were small. You see, I'm so busy . . .'

'*You're* so busy! It's all me me, isn't it?' Chris's anger burst out. 'How do you think *she* feels – stuck at home with nothing to do but clean *your* house and iron *your* shirts? Has it ever occurred to you, Mike, that your wife might be lonely? That she might find married life less fulfilling, less fun than working on an oncology ward?'

Michael opened his mouth, and then shut it again. Chris was very quiet for a minute. It was his turn to look at his shoes. 'I apologise,' he said. 'I had no right to speak to you like that. I'm sorry. Perhaps I should go.'

'No, Chris. Don't go. Please don't go.' Michael was pleading now. 'You're absolutely right. I've been a selfish bastard. I just assumed that my work was more important than Jane's. I took it for granted that she should stay at home and look after the kids – and I didn't even notice that she was becoming more and more withdrawn. I was too preoccupied with myself, my work, my fantasy life. Please. Please will you help me to sort my life out. I really love Jane. I want her to be happy. Please help.'

Chris stood up. 'Can I let you know, Mike?' he said coolly. 'I'll give you a ring in a day or two. Now, if you'll forgive me, I'll just pop up and see Jane for a moment.'

It was just half past eight the following morning when Chris's car pulled up outside Susie's house. The door was opened by her husband Ben who led him through to the kitchen where Susie was finishing her breakfast. She looked up. 'Hi, Chris,' she said. 'Come in. I won't be a moment. Pour yourself a coffee.'

Chris helped himself and sat down. What a god-awful time to have supervision he thought – but they'd been through this before. It was the only time they could be sure of some uninterrupted space and Susie Wellington, at 50 plus, was acknowledged to be the best psychotherapist in the region and the shrewdest supervisor available. Chris knew he was lucky to have regular time with her.

'Well, Chris?' said Susie as they settled down in her study. 'What have we got this week?' She looked at him expectantly.

Chris shifted a little in his seat. This wasn't going to be easy. Working with colleagues never was and bringing them as material for supervision was particularly delicate. He took a deep breath. 'It's about a colleague,' he said, 'and I don't quite know where I am or if I should pull out before I get any more involved. Also, it's touched me somewhere on the raw and I can't quite work out what's happening.'

Susie said nothing. She knew Chris well and respected him deeply. He was a particularly sensitive and skilled psychiatrist whose growing self awareness of his own psychological processes was deepening his skills as a therapist. Still Chris said nothing but she was quite relaxed. She was far too experienced a therapist to fall into the trap of filling a silent void just because she felt uncomfortable. Chris would speak when he was ready and she was happy to wait for him.

'It's like this,' said Chris, jumping into space. 'I have a friend who's a GP. He's about my age. Most of our contact has been professional, so I don't know his wife all that well. Anyway, last week I was doing a supervision session for a couple of people, and at the end of the session one of them asked to see me on my own. She's the nurse at my friend's practice and it turned out that she and some of the others were worried about him.'

'What was bothering them?' asked Susie.

'I was coming to that. He'd been irritable and hard to work with for the past few weeks and then, one day, the receptionist found him crying when she took his coffee in. Caroline, that's the nurse, knew that we were friends and asked if I could intervene. She was particularly concerned because the receptionist, who I gather is a shrewd lady, thought my friend was in trouble with his marriage.'

'Sticky one that.' Susie was sympathetic. 'What did you do?'

'Well, as things turned out, I didn't have to engineer anything, because I was asked to see my friend's wife professionally because she was depressed.'

'Was that a problem?'

'No. Not at all. That was quite straightforward. What I want to discuss is the feelings that have been stirred up by a session I had with her husband last night. I went back to the house after work and had a longish talk. Initially it was fine – there was an issue of infidelity that I felt fairly confident to handle, but then something else emerged and I found myself getting really angry. I actually lashed out at him verbally in a way which I regretted immediately, and then, well frankly, I just wanted to run away.'

'And did you?'

'Well, sort of. I brought the session to a premature conclusion and left him pretty miserable.'

'Do you want to talk about what made you angry?' asked Susie.

'Yes,' said Chris slowly. 'I think I must, because it's stirred up a whole hornets' nest of emotions for me and I have to decide whether to continue working with them or whether to pass them on to a colleague.'

'Go on.'

'Well, I suppose we were about half an hour into the conversation. He'd been very frank about the infidelity issue and I think I handled that okay. Then I had a hunch that there was something more fundamental wrong in his relationship with his wife. At first I thought it was the usual problem of him working too hard and not being home enough and then it emerged that he hadn't really got a clue how his wife spent her day apart from running his home and looking after his kids. It turns out she was quite a high powered nurse and that she probably wants to go back to part time work but *he* won't have it because he thinks a wife's place is in the home.'

'How did you feel about this?'

'Frankly, I wanted to shake him till his teeth rattled. I thought you selfish bastard. You're so full of your own professional importance and your own sexual fantasies that you've let your wife get so depressed that she's suicidal – and you haven't even noticed.'

'Got you on the raw, hasn't it,' said Susie gently.

'You could say so,' Chris grinned.

'Where's it coming from? Have you worked that out yet?'

'I've been trying,' said Chris, 'I imagine it comes from my father. He was a doctor, a country GP'.

Susie nodded, 'That would figure. What about your mother?'

44

'She looked after us.'

'And answered the phone,' said Susie, 'and warmed your father's slippers?'

'If you put it like that, yes.' Chris felt uncomfortable.

'And how did she feel about it?' asked Susie.

'I don't know. She never said.'

'Is she still alive?'

'Oh yes,' said Chris, more animated now. 'Very much so. She was quite a lot younger than my father. He died of a coronary about ten years ago and she started working again.'

'Back to work?'

'Yes,' said Chris. 'She was a writer. She's published several books since he died.'

'So, that's where your creativity comes from!' Susie smiled. 'I always thought you had some special genes locked away somewhere! Did she do any writing while your father was alive?'

'No, not really. She always said she hadn't got the space.'

'The space?'

'The interior, emotional space. You see, we lived about the shop: the surgery was attached to the house, so father was in and out all day and the phone rang non-stop.'

'What sort of a man was your father?'

Chris was silent while he thought. 'Do you know, no one's ever asked me that before. I suppose he was a pretty demanding sort of person. He never stopped working. The patients adored him. Thought of him as some sort of saint.'

'And your mother?' asked Susie quietly. 'How was their relationship?'

'It's difficult to say.' Chris was tentative. 'Pretty formal, I think. He wasn't a man to show a lot of affection. He was always too busy being the perfect doctor.'

'How was your relationship with him?'

'Oh I worshipped the ground he walked on,' said Chris quickly. 'He was always my hero. He's the reason I did medicine.'

'And now? How do you feel about him?'

'I'm not sure. Something seems to be shifting.'

'Shifting?' said Susie.

'Yes. I feel as though something's moving deep in my unconscious. I think I'm starting to question my own status quo.'

45

'The way you are now?'

'No,' he said. 'The past. The model I've had of my childhood. My memory of a wonderful father and a happy mother.'

'That could be hard,' said Susie quietly.

'It is already. You see, I'm not sure any more that my mother *was* happy. She's changed so dramatically since my father died.'

'Changed?' said Susie. 'In what way?'

'She's more alive. She's vibrant. She's full of energy and laughter.' Chris paused for a moment. 'Do you know,' he said, 'I think she's much happier. She strikes me as being an incredibly free spirit.'

'Are you saying your father had her in a cage?' Chris thought for a moment, then he said, 'Those are your words not mine. But I think you're right. Maybe my father wasn't so wonderful after all. Maybe he was a selfish bastard too, like my friend the GP.'

'How does that feel?' asked Susie quietly.

'Scary. As I said before, my ground is shifting, cracking under my feet. What do I do, Susie?'

'What *can* you do?' she asked.

'Well, I can't go back,' he said slowly, 'that's for sure. I suppose I've got to face it. Live with it till I've processed it.'

Susie nodded gravely, and Chris was silent for a minute. 'Time's moving. What do I do with my clients?' he asked. 'Stay with them or pass them on?'

Susie was not going to make Chris's decision for him. 'What do *you* think?' she said.

'Damn,' said Chris. 'I think I should stay with it. I'm in too deep. They wouldn't understand if I backed off. I think they need me.'

'Can you handle it?' she asked.

Chris nodded, 'I think so.'

'Sure?'

'No,' he grinned, 'but I'll try.'

'Ring me if you need to.'

Chris smiled warmly. 'Thanks Susie. See you in two weeks. Bye.'

When he got to the office, Chris rang Michael. 'Hello, Mike,' he said. How's things?'

'Oh, Chris. Thanks for ringing. Jane's had a really good night. She's a bit sleepy this morning, but she's had some breakfast.'

'And you?'

'Not so good. I've had a pretty miserable night, thinking about our conversation. I feel a right shit.'

Chris's voice was warm: 'Don't be too hard on yourself,' he said. 'Now, when shall we meet again? How about Friday evening, six o'clock, at my office.'

'So, you're prepared to see me?'

'We'll give it a go, Mike. See you Friday. Ring me if you need to. Goodbye.' Michael put down the telephone and the tears ran freely down his cheeks.

8

'It's Sarah Westward, the oncology social worker, Dr Walker,' said Karen. 'Are you free to speak to her?'

'Oh, yes. Put her through, please, Karen. Chris's voice was warm, 'Sarah? What can I do for you?'

'Chris? Sorry to trouble you,' said Sarah, 'but I hear you're seeing Katie and Emma this afternoon.'

'Yes. At four. Any problems?'

'No,' said Sarah. 'I just thought you might like to be updated about Katie.'

'Yes please. Let me find a pen.' Chris searched for his pen, buried under a pile of letters and, grabbing an empty envelope from his waste paper basket, said, 'Right. Tell.'

'Well, I saw her yesterday and we were talking about arrangements for her children when suddenly the flood gates opened and there was no stopping her. It seems her mother died when she was nine and her father married again two years later. The new stepmother didn't like Katie – was jealous of her, and was always finding fault and trying to get her father to discipline her.'

'And?'

'Well he did, and,' Sarah hesitated, 'it sounds as though he rather enjoyed it.'

'Meaning?'

'Oh it's a very messy story,' she said. 'He managed to combine physical and sexual abuse until Katie didn't know whether he loved her or hated her. He really messed her up.'

'Did you tell her you were going to phone me?'

'Yes. I asked her if she'd mind my telling you a bit about her.'

'And she agreed?' Chris sounded mildly surprised.

'Yes. It seems she was really impressed by how you managed to tame young Emma, so she's prepared to trust you.'

'Well – that should make things easier. Is there anything else I should know?'

'I don't think so.' Sarah thought for a moment. 'We spent a lot of time talking about her father. She needed to cry and I just sat there with her.'

'Well done, Sarah,' said Chris warmly. 'When's the operation?'

'It's been postponed while we sort out care for the children,' said Sarah.

'Fine. So I've got a bit of time to work with her and Emma. Thanks Sarah. I'll be in touch.'

'Hello, Emma,' Chris smiled. 'And this must be your mum?' He extended his hand to the tall, good looking young woman at Emma's side. 'Good afternoon, Mrs Roberts.'

Katie smiled nervously. She'd never met a psychiatrist before.

'Emma,' said Chris, 'will you be happy to wait here while I talk to your mum?'

Emma grinned sheepishly. 'I've brought my homework' she said.

'Well done,' said Chris. 'I'm sure Karen will give you a hand if you need it!'

'So long as it's not Maths!' retorted Karen spiritedly, 'I've never been any good at sums!'

When he and Katie had settled themselves in the consulting room, Chris looked straight at her. 'How can I help you?' he said gently.

Katie was puzzled. She thought she'd come to talk about Emma, not about herself. 'I'm not sure,' she said diffidently.

Chris waited for a moment, and when it seemed that Katie wasn't going to volunteer anything, decided on another tack. 'Why don't I tell you what I know so far,' he said gently, 'and then we needn't necessarily cover old ground.' Katie looked apprehensive. Has Sarah spoken to him already? she thought. What must he think of me?

'I've spoken to Sarah this morning,' said Chris, 'and she's told me about your mother's death and about the difficulties with your father.'

Katie looked down at her lap and bit her lip. Chris was very gentle: 'You had a really rough childhood, didn't you? How did you feel towards your father?'

Katie's eyes remained fixed on to her lap. She wasn't used to people being so kind. If I look him in the eye I shall fall apart.

49

I'll just howl, and then what will he think of me? Slowly Katie realised that Chris was waiting for an answer. She struggled to remember his question. '*Feel* about him?' she said, 'When? When he was beating me? When he was amusing himself? When?'

'I meant in general, Katie. Do you mind if I call you by your first name?' Chris said.

'No,' Katie paused, as though searching for the right words. 'I think I was totally confused,' she said. 'Basically, I adored him. He was my life, my hero. My protector. We had a wonderful relationship until my Mum died and he married my stepmother. I was 12, and very possessive of my dad. I was fiendishly jealous of my stepmother and she really hated me. I played her up something terrible and she was always telling my father to beat me. *She* couldn't catch me. I could run faster than her any day. Anyway, one day my dad decided that I needed to be taught a lesson and he took me to my room and, and . . .'

'Take your time.'

'He put me over his knee to spank me, and . . . and when he'd done it he kept me there and he began, he began to touch me.'

'How did that make you feel Katie?'

'At first I was very upset and struggled to get away, but then, then it began to feel good, so I just lay there . . .' Katie was crying now. What must he think of me. Why on earth did I tell him that. He'll think I'm a pervert. Katie felt something soft touch her hand – the doctor was passing her a handful of tissues. She gulped. 'Thanks.'

'Katie – would you like a coffee?' said Chris. 'I think I'll make one for myself.' Katie nodded, barely able to speak.

By the time Chris returned with the coffee, Katie had recovered some of her composure. 'I'm sorry,' she said.

'Sorry?' said Chris. 'Why?'

'To burden you with all that – all that shit.'

'Katie,' said Chris gently, 'that's what I'm here for. Tell me, when you're ready, how you feel about it all now.'

'Now? Right this minute I feel really dirty.'

Chris sighed. If only these men *knew* what they were laying on their kids, he thought angrily. 'Why dirty?' he said, very gently.

'Because I *enjoyed* it. That's why. I loved my father and I *liked* the way I felt when he touched me. That's incest. You can't get

50

much dirtier than that can you?' Katie looked up at Chris, her face strained with tears. I don't know how I can live with myself,' she said bitterly. 'Anyway, now I'm being punished, aren't I? I've got what's coming to me.'

'Katie,' Chris's voice was firmer, full of a quiet authority. 'Katie, I want you to listen to me for a moment while I explain something to you. What your father did to you was very wrong. I know you were naughty and that your stepmother egged him on, but you were far too old to be spanked in that way. It's no wonder that you were sexually aroused by what he did. Your father was abusing his power over you. He was betraying your love and your trust. Do you understand?' Katie nodded and Chris continued.

'Things that happen to us when we're children can have effects which last all our lives. I spend a lot of my time trying to help men and women, particularly women, who have been hurt in the way you have.'

'What can you do?' said Katie, 'You can't undo the past.'

'No, but I can try and undo some of the chains which bind you – the chains of guilt and shame which are stopping you from functioning as you should.'

'Do *you* think that the cancer is God's punishment on me?'

'No, Katie, I don't,' said Chris decisively. 'I am quite, quite sure that it isn't.'

'But they say cancer of the cervix is associated with having sex too early and having lots of partners,' said Katie.

'That's true,' Chris acknowledged, 'but it's a lot more compli-cated than that. It still doesn't mean that God is punishing you for being abused by your father . . .' He paused.

Katie still looked doubtful.

'Katie,' said Chris, 'I don't know if there *is* a God, but if there is I am quite, quite sure that he or she would not punish you in this way. It would be completely unjust, because you have done nothing wrong.'

Katie smiled through her tears. 'I'd like to believe you,' she said.

'Well, will you please try?' said Chris smiling back at her. 'I'm exhausted with trying to convince you!'

'Okay,' she said with a new conviction in her voice. 'I believe!'

'Sure?' said Chris. Katie nodded.

'Good. Now, Katie, there are other things we have to talk about.'

'I know,' said Katie. 'What about Emma?'

'Did she tell you anything about our conversation?'

'Not really. She just said you were wonderful and that you really listened to her.'

'I'm glad. Now Katie, I'm afraid what I've got to say isn't going to be easy, so please hear me out.'

Katie looked anxiously at Chris. 'She's sleeping with her boy-friend,' she said, 'that Joe, isn't she?'

'Yes,' said Chris, 'that's true, but there's more to it than that.'

'More? What do you mean?'

'I mean that Emma was being abused by her father in much the same way as you were.'

'By Adam?' Katie was white with anger. 'The bastard. The dirty bastard. Poor little tyke. Are you sure? She told me that years ago, but I thought she was lying.'

'Well, I'm as sure as I can be that it's true,' said Chris, 'and we need to sort something out before you go into hospital.'

'Of course. No wonder she refused to go to her father at weekends.'

'What'll you do while you're in hospital Katie,' said Chris quietly, 'and what about the other two children?'

'I've got a friend, a really good friend. She's going to come and look after the kids and stay with me till I'm strong enough to cope.'

'Have you been in contact with her?' asked Chris. 'Are you sure she can come?'

'Yes.' Katie was confident now. 'I phoned her after lunch today and she's coming next week.'

'That's really good. I'm so pleased. Chris looked up at Katie. 'Well, that was a lot for one afternoon,' he said smiling. 'Well done.'

Katie grinned. 'I'm strong,' she said. 'I've had to be.' Chris smiled. 'I'd like to see you once more before your operation, if that's all right. One day next week.'

Katie smiled. 'Thanks,' she said. 'I'd like that.'

9

'Hello,' said Katie. 'My name's Katie Roberts. What's yours?' 'Mary,' said Mary, grateful for the other woman's warmth. She felt sick with apprehension: John had just left and she and Katie sat with four or five other women in the day room of Nightingale Ward in the Royal Victoria Hospital waiting to be shown to their beds. Katie looked closely at Mary and was surprised at how scared she looked.

Her musing was interrupted by the arrival of Staff Nurse Andrea Buckley, a plump cheerful girl in her mid-twenties. 'Good morning ladies,' she said. 'Sister's on days off today, so you'll have to make do with me! My name's Andrea and I'd like to welcome you to Nightingale Ward – one of the wards in the Department of Women's Services. Now, we work in two teams here, the red and the blue team. The red team works mainly with Mr Dalton and the blue team with Mr Giles. Each of you will have a nurse assigned to you, and she will be responsible for making sure you get everything you need.' Andrea looked down at her list. 'Mrs Carlisle and Miss Roberts: Debbie will be your nurse, so if you'd like to go with her, she'll show you to your beds. We'd like you to put on your night clothes please, because the house doctors will be coming to see you soon.'

'God,' said Katie, grinning, 'This is just like boarding school – I feel about ten!'

Mary bit her lip and managed a smile. 'I feel homesick,' she said. 'I want my mummy!'

'Go on,' said Katie, 'It'll be fun! I bet they have midnight feasts!'

Mary tried hard to join in the game but all she could raise was a weak smile. Katie, deciding that frivolity was getting her nowhere, said gently, 'Are you scared?'

Mary gulped, fighting back the tears. 'Yes,' she said. 'Very. You see, I've never been in hospital before, not even to have my babies.'

'Oh it's not too bad. They're usually pretty kind.'

'What are you having done?'

'A hysterectomy. What about you?'

'A mastectomy. I've got breast cancer.'

'That's tough. I'm sorry. I thought you didn't have to have the breast off these days? I thought they just cut the cancer out?'

'That's what we'd hoped, but apparently mine is affecting the whole breast, so I have to have it off.' She paused. 'Why are you having a hysterectomy: surely you're very young for that. Are your periods too heavy or something?'

'I've got cancer too.' Katie's voice was quiet now. 'Oh.' Mary sounded surprised. 'You too. You look so healthy.'

'So do you,' Katie retorted. Then, sorry that she'd been sharp said, 'God, it spooks me out of my mind. The bloody thing growing there, eating you away, and you never know a thing about it till . . .'

'Go on, say it: till it's too late.'

'What's too late, ladies?' It was Debbie, their 'team nurse'. Katie and Mary looked at each other, sensing instinctively that they shouldn't be talking about their cancers. Katie looked at the cheerful young nurse. Damn. Why shouldn't we talk about it. Why should we keep up a polite façade?

'We were talking about cancer,' said Katie firmly. 'How it creeps up on you, and you never know it's there until it's too late.'

'Too late,' said Debbie, suddenly very serious. 'Who says it's too late?'

'Well,' said Mary, 'all you ever hear is about the people who die of it. You never hear of anyone getting better!'

Debbie looked calmly at Mary. 'You know, Mrs Carlisle . . . Do you mind if I call you Mary? You know, that's just not true. If you get it early enough, cancer can often be cured. Did you know there's a 95 per cent cure rate in some cancers? That's why early diagnosis is so important. That's why we have screening programmes.'

Katie was looking really interested now. 'What about cancer of the cervix?' she said. 'Do you think I could be cured?'

'I'm afraid you'll have to talk to the doctor about your own particular situation, Katie. He'll be along quite soon. Now, Mary, could you pop into bed for a minute or two: Mr Giles is doing his ward round and he may want to examine you.'

'But he examined me on Wednesday.'

'I know,' said Debbie firmly, 'But he may need to do so again.'

What's wrong? Mary wondered why he would want to examine her again. Surely it can't have grown since last week? Mary took off her dressing gown and climbed into bed, feeling rather foolish to be in her nightie, at half past ten in the morning.

'What about me?' Katie looked enquiringly at the nurse.

'You can wait till the house officer comes,' she said. 'He's in theatre at the moment and he may be a while.' Debbie looked towards the door. 'Oh,' she said, 'here's Mr Giles.'

Tony Giles smiled as he approached Mary's bed. 'Hello Mrs Carlisle,' he said. 'How are you feeling?'

'Not too bad thanks.' Mary's voice was uncertain.

She's *so* scared, this woman. He sat on Mary's bed and spoke to her very quietly: 'Try not to worry,' he said, 'I'm sorry we've got to take the breast off, but as I explained, it really is necessary.'

Mary nodded, as ever, close to tears.

'You'll be first on the list tomorrow morning and when you wake up you'll have a big firm bandage on your chest and a drain running into a bottle. The anaesthetist will come and see you this evening and he'll explain about the anaesthetic and your pain control after the operation.' He paused. 'Is there anything you wanted to ask me?'

Mary hesitated. She looked down at her hands, then, plucking up all her courage said, 'I will be all right, won't I? I mean, you have caught it in time?'

Tony Giles took his time. How difficult it was to know what was the right thing to say. When he spoke, his words were measured: 'We'll do everything we can to make you better, but I can't promise to cure you. There's a very good chance that we'll be able to take all the tumour away. We just have to cross our fingers and hope.'

Mary smiled at him. 'Thank you,' she said weakly, 'I'm sorry to be so anxious.'

'Goodbye then. I'll see you tomorrow before your operation.'

Mary was very quiet when the surgeon had gone. Katie looked at her thoughtfully. Rather you than me, mate. I don't know how I'd cope with losing a breast.

The two women sat in silence for a while, but then their reverie was interrupted by Debbie who arrived with a middle-aged woman in a white dress. 'Mary,' she said. 'This is Tessa

Metcalfe, the breast care nurse. She'll be helping you after the operation, with finding the right prosthesis, bras and things.' There was a kind, down-to-earth quality to Debbie's approach that Mary found strangely comforting. Everyone seemed so relaxed, so quietly confident in what they said and did, as if they did it every day. She looked up at the breast nurse, a comfortable looking woman with a large, maternal bosom. She looked as though she'd understand about what breasts mean to a woman, about Mary's worries about looking lopsided and ugly.

'Hello,' said Tessa, 'I thought we'd go and talk in my office, away from all the noise and bustle. How would that be?'

'Now?' said Mary.

'Sure, if that's okay by you?'

Mary climbed out of bed and tied up her dressing gown.

'Would you like to bring your bra along,' said Tessa, 'so we can see how it fits and things.'

Mary scrabbled in her locker, wishing that she'd bought a new bra – this one had that grubby grey look that nylon seems to take on however often you wash it.

Mary was just wondering what Tessa would think of her when the other women said softly: 'It would be good if you've brought a comfy old one, so we know what really fits.'

Mary smiled and shoving the bra into the pocket of her dressing gown stood up and waited expectantly.

'All set, Mary? Shall we go then?'

'Bye. See you later,' said Katie, and Mary turned round and smiled realising suddenly that she had a new friend.

'It's a real rabbit warren, this, isn't it?' said Tessa, as she led Mary down a series of corridors. 'It took me weeks to find my way around and even now I get lost sometimes!' Mary felt increasingly comfy with Tessa: she was so friendly and down-to-earth. At last they arrived at a door labelled Mrs T. Metcalfe. Counsellor. Women's Services.

'Come in,' said Tessa. 'Do have a seat. Would you like a coffee?'

'Yes please.'

Tessa handed Mary her coffee and, sitting down herself took a deep draught.

'Ah! I needed that.' She paused a moment as though to collect her thoughts. 'So – how are you feeling about things?'

Yet again Mary felt the tears coming. This woman was so friendly. She tried to say 'not too bad' but the words stuck in her throat. She felt in her pocket for her hanky but found herself holding her bra instead. This indignity was one last straw and she began to sob, her shoulders hunched and her head bowed. Her tears flowed in a great torrent and she felt she would choke. As if by magic, some tissues appeared in her hand and she held them to her eyes, but still the tears came. Gradually, she became aware of an arm around her shoulders and she realised that Tessa was kneeling beside her.

'Come on, love, let it out. It's got to come out. Just let go.'

Mary turned towards the voice and found herself in Tessa's arms, with her head buried in that ample friendly bosom. Tessa's knees began to ache, and she wished yet again that the health service would use better quality underlay under their carpets. Quietly, she held the woman until the sobbing died away and Mary herself began to straighten up and dry her eyes.

'Okay?'

Mary smiled, 'Thanks.'

'Have some more coffee, and then we'll talk.'

Mary took a long gulp of her coffee and then looked up expectantly at the woman opposite her.

'Mary,' Tessa's voice was firmer now. 'I think we need to try to get at just what it is that is making you so desperate. Is it the fact of having cancer, or that you're going to lose your breast, or is it all that and more besides?'

'I think it's all that,' said Mary, 'but I'm so mixed up, I can't think straight.'

'Well, suppose we take things one at a time. Can you identify which is the most urgent issue for you – not necessarily the most important, but the most pressing.'

Mary thought hard. 'Right now,' she said, 'it's the fact that I'm going to lose my breast. It's just hitting me that this time tomorrow it will have gone, and I'll be deformed, mutilated, ugly, for ever.'

'So, we'll look at that first. But before we start, I'd like to you to try and think what other things are bothering you, and we'll deal with those later.'

Mary looked down at her hands, still clutching a sodden tissue. 'I'm afraid,' she said. 'I'm afraid of everything. I'm afraid of the hospital, of the doctors, of the operation, of the pain. And I'm afraid . . . I'm afraid they won't be able to cure me, that the cancer will come back. That I'm going to die.'

'That's a big one, isn't it,' said Tessa, 'and it's not an easy one to exorcise. Anything else?'

Mary thought. 'No, I don't think so. When I first discovered the lump I got in a terrible stew that John, my husband, would leave me, but I'm fine about that now.'

'He's been supportive?'

'He's been wonderful. I don't think I could have coped without him.'

'That's good.'

'Do you have children?'

'Yes. A boy and a girl. Lisa's eleven and Jamie's seven.'

'Have you told them about the cancer?'

'No, not yet. I thought it best not to worry them till we had to.'

'I see. Maybe we'll talk more about that another day. What I'd like to do now is look with you at what it means to you to lose one of your breasts.'

Mary looked at Tessa but said nothing.

'Now,' she said, 'I'd like to do a simple exercise with you.' Taking a large sheet of paper, she placed it on the coffee table in the centre of the room, and wrote, in large letters with a red felt tip pen, the word BREAST. Mary tensed up automatically.

'Now, Mary, I want you to say to me all the words that come into your head when you think of the word breast. Just off the top of your head. Don't think it through: just say it.'

Mary sat very still. Her mouth was dry. At last, pulling herself together she said, 'WOMAN.'

'Fine. Go on,' said Tessa as she wrote the word WOMAN on the paper. 'CHILD,' said Mary, 'BABY. FEEDING. SUCKLE. LOVE.'

'Well done. You've got the hang of it.'

Mary paused then, she blurted out, 'LOVE. SEX. FEMI-NINITY.'

Tessa worked quickly, writing the words down in a cluster around the original BREAST. 'Go on.'

'I can't think of any more.'

'Try. Think of tomorrow.'

Suddenly Mary was angry. 'MASTECTOMY,' she almost shouted. 'KNIFE. MEN. ABUSE. MUTILATION.'

'Okay,' Tessa was very quiet now. 'Anything else?'

Mary shook her head.

'Let's just look at it quietly for a moment.'

The two women sat in silence for a minute or so, their eyes fixed on the piece of paper. Then, looking up at Mary, Tessa said gently, 'Which one of those words is most significant for you at the moment Mary? Not which one you think *ought* to be most important, but the one that really is.'

Mary looked down again at her hands and said in a small voice, 'FEMININITY . . . LOVE. SEX. JOHN.'

'So what do you think will happen to your femininity when you lose your breast?'

'I'll be less of a woman. I'll be mutilated. My body will be ugly. John won't find me beautiful any more.'

Tessa listened carefully. 'Your breasts are very important to you, aren't they Mary?'

Mary nodded. 'I know I'm stupid,' she said, 'but you see, I know I'm not very beautiful, but I've always had a good figure, and my husband gets very aroused by my breasts. He loves looking at them, touching them, holding them.'

Tessa nodded comfortably. 'I understand' she said. 'You *do* have a lovely figure but what about you yourself Mary? How important are your breasts to *you*? Do you enjoy them?'

Mary thought. 'I suppose they reassure me that I'm desirable, that I'm a woman.'

'Okay,' said Tessa. 'I understand that. You're not unusual here. Many women feel as you do. But what about women with small breasts? What about those who are really flat chested? Do you think of them as less feminine than yourself?'

'No,' said Mary. 'Of course not. I know that women come in all shapes and sizes. My sister-in-law, Ellen, is very flat chested, but she's incredibly feminine, really sexy.'

'That's interesting. Have you ever wondered what it is that makes Ellen so feminine and sexy?'

'Well,' said Mary, 'she's warm and gentle and lively, a really lovely personality. She dresses well too, and she's a wonderful mother. Somehow she just attracts men to her, and she really enjoys their company. She's *all* woman.'

'Yet she has small breasts?'

'Tiny really. She always laughs that the only time she's had a bosom is when she's been pregnant.'

'So it's not Ellen's breast which make her feminine, sexy, attractive to her husband?'

'No, of course not.'

'So, what about you?'

'*What* about me?'

'Could it be that your breasts are just a part of who you are, actually quite a small part, and it's the person that you are that's really important?' There was a long pause while Mary considered what Tessa was saying.

Then she nodded. 'I see what you're getting at.'

'Am I right?'

Mary straightened up. 'Of course you're right,' she said firmly. 'I've got things all out of proportion, haven't I?'

'Perhaps you have. But you're not the only one. A lot of women think like you.'

'And how do they get over it?'

'They learn, as you are learning, to understand what it really means to be feminine, what it means to be a woman: that a woman is more than her body, that physical beauty is a passing gift, that it's the spirit that matters.'

'Thank you,' said Mary, quietly. 'That was very helpful.'

'I'm glad.' Tessa smiled. 'Have you had enough now, or do you want to talk through the other issues?'

'I think maybe I've had enough for the moment,' said Mary. 'I need to digest what you've said.'

'That's fine,' said Tessa. 'But before you go I'd like to have a look at you and your bra so that I can be thinking about getting a prosthesis for you. Do you mind if I examine your breasts?'

Mary took off her dressing gown and then, slowly and awkwardly, took off her night-dress until she was standing there in only her pants.

Tessa smiled at her. 'Do you feel shy?'

Mary nodded.

'Try not to. This is my job, I do it every day.' Standing in front of Mary she looked straight at her with a professional eye. 'Could you put your hands on your head please, Mary. Fine, now on your hips.'

Mary stood there uncomfortably, cursing her prudish Catholic upbringing in which the body was regarded as something shameful, to be covered at all costs. Now, Tessa was touching her, lifting each breast in her hand, feeling the weight of it. 'Right. Could you put your bra on now, please.'

Mary did as she was asked, regretting once again that the bra was old and looked distinctly grubby. Once more Tessa examined her, checking the fit of the garment and the tension of the shoulder straps. At last she was finished. 'Right,' she said. 'That's it. Could you leave your bra with me, Mary? It will help me to choose the best prosthesis for you.'

'Of course.' Mary paused. 'The prosthesis . . . what's it like? I mean what does it *feel* like. Can you tell that it's false.'

'I was coming to that. Why don't we sit down again for a few minutes while I tell you all about it.'

Mary sat down, trying hard to relax.

'Now,' said Tessa, reaching in a drawer behind her. 'This is a temporary prosthesis which you wear as soon as the wound has healed.' She handed her a flesh coloured object, soft, and wobbly which only vaguely resembled a human breast.

Mary took it gingerly in her hands. 'It's heavy,' she said in surprise.

Tessa smiled. 'Of course it's heavy,' she said. 'A breast is heavy, isn't it? If you don't have a prosthesis of the right weight, you'll feel lopsided and uncomfortable.'

'Of course.' Mary grinned. 'I'm sorry to be so dense.'

'It's all right, you're doing fine.' Tessa handed a different pink object. 'Now, this is what we call a definitive prosthesis – one that is matched as nearly as possible to your own breast. You wear this with your own bra. You can take it swimming, wear it with an evening dress, anything. No one can possibly tell by looking at you that you don't have two normal breasts.'

'Are you sure? It can't fall out?'

'You'd make history if it did!'

'Right. I believe you!'

'Good. I think that's enough for one day. I'll come and see

you again a couple of days after your op and see how you're feeling. Good luck for tomorrow.'

Mary faced Tessa and then, shyly she took her hand. 'Thank you *so* much,' she said. 'You've been very kind.'

Tessa smiled. 'How about a hug?' she said, and, enfolding Mary in her arms held her there comfortably until the other woman was ready to move away.

10

Katie was quite composed as she sat facing the gynaecologist in the examination room on Nightingale Ward. She was glad the doctor was a woman and that she had been gentle in her examination.

'What are my chances, doctor?' she said. 'I'm a single mother and I need to know.'

Liz Townsend looked at the open faced young woman before her and her heart warmed. This was a woman after her own heart: a straightforward, no nonsense woman struggling to remain in control of her life and future. She smiled and said in her broad Australian accent: 'I think you'll be fine, Katie. Your disease is at an early stage and I see no reason why we shouldn't eradicate it completely.'

'Thank you,' said Katie. 'I knew you wouldn't lie to me.'

'No, Katie. I never lie and if I was in your shoes I'd make damn sure no one lied to me. Now, before you go, is there anything you'd like to ask me? Do you have any concerns?'

Katie thought and then said, 'What about sex? Will I still want to? And will it be okay?'

'I'm glad you asked.' Liz was very matter of fact. 'There should be no problem. We'll be removing your ovaries, so you will, in effect, have a premature menopause, but we'll start you on HRT – hormone replacement therapy – right away so we shouldn't get any oestrogen withdrawal symptoms. You should be able to return to normal sexual relationships when everything's healed up. Do you have a partner?'

Katie grimaced. 'He walked out, the bastard. Couldn't stand the fact that I was sick.'

'I'm sorry.' Liz was very gentle now. 'Would it help to talk about it?'

'Thanks,' said Katie, 'but I'm fine really. Just sad and a bit bitter. I got a lot of help from a psychiatrist I saw last week. He's helping to sort out my teenage daughter and he seems to have adopted me as well.'

'I'm glad you've got someone to talk to. This operation affects different women in different ways. Some people find it quite devastating to lose their womb, to think that they can never have children again. Some of them feel very threatened, that they will be somehow less feminine, only half a woman, and that it will be written all over their faces.'

Katie smiled. 'No,' she said. 'I've got no problems of that sort. I also know the difference between my uterus and my ovaries. I'm thankful about the HRT though, as it would have been hard to accept the menopause at 29.'

'You're right there. It's been a real breakthrough that. It's transformed a lot of women's lives. They're healthier, more energetic, and, what's really important, they're protected from osteoporosis – thinning of the bones.'

'What about the risk of breast cancer? The woman in the bed next to mine had a mastectomy this morning. She's absolutely shit scared.'

'There's no clear evidence that women on HRT are more at risk than other women unless they've been on it for more than ten years when there might be a very small risk. What we do know, though, is that use of oestrogen, that is oestrogen without progesterone, in women with a uterus carries an increased risk of cancer of the endometrium or the lining of the uterus. That's why anyone on HRT who hasn't had a hysterectomy is always given a combined preparation of oestrogen and a progesterone. Are you with me?'

'Yes, I think so. But this doesn't apply to me, does it, because I'm having a hysterectomy?'

'That's right.' Liz looked at her watch. 'Anything else, Katie?'

Katie smiled. 'No thanks. That was really helpful. Thank you for being so open with me.'

'No problem, Katie. We're pretty forthright where I come from! Goodbye for now. I must be off. I'll see you in theatre on Monday,' and with a wide smile and a shake of her red hair, Liz was gone.

Mary's bed was still empty when Katie returned to the ward. Worried about her new friend, she sought out Debbie who was taking round the medicine trolley.

'How's Mary?'

Debbie smiled. 'She's fine. She's in the post-op observation ward at the moment but she'll be back with you tomorrow.'

'Oh, good,' said Katie. 'Thanks.'

'No problem.' Debbie smiled and returned her attention to her trolley with its charts and bottles.

'May I go for a walk down the corridor?' Katie was diffident. One never knew what the rules were, although this ward seemed very relaxed.

'Sure. You've seen Dr Townsend, haven't you? Don't go too far. We want you to be rested for tomorrow.'

Katie smiled. 'Don't worry,' she said, 'I won't run away!'

Katie put on her trousers and a sweatshirt and set out in search of adventure. The ward was quiet and the corridor outside even quieter, with the weekend peace that overcomes the busiest hospital when routine work ceases and emergencies are few.

Feeling in need of exercise, Katie went down two flights of stairs and along the wide corridor identical to the one in which her own ward was located. As she walked down the corridor, she noticed a young man in pyjamas and dressing gown standing by the window. He turned as she approached and she saw that his face was pale and drawn.

'Hello,' she said. 'Admiring the view?'

'No,' he said. 'Wondering about jumping out.'

Katie did a double take and he smiled.

'Sorry,' he said, 'Sick joke.'

Katie was quiet for a moment, and then she said softly, 'But you meant it, didn't you.'

Robbie looked her straight in the eye. 'Yes,' he said, 'I did.'

'Do you want to tell me why?'

'What's the use? Are you another bloody counsellor?'

'No,' said Katie. 'I'm a patient like you. I've just been let out for a walk. I'm having an operation tomorrow.'

'Oh,' said Robbie. 'Sorry. Well, it's either that or jumping and I don't think I could do that in front of a lady!'

'How about a coffee?'

'You're on. Have you got any money?'

Katie felt in the pocket of her trousers. 'Two quid,' she said.

'We're rich. Let's go down to the canteen. We'll take the lift if you don't mind. I don't feel up to stairs.'

'You obviously know your way around this place,' said Katie as they settled themselves at a table in the corner of the canteen. 'Been here long?'

'Not long this time. But I've been here so often it feels like home. The trouble about me topping myself is that the nurses would feel they'd failed me.'

'Failed you? How come?'

'Failed to support me, failed to help me face the fact that I'm going to die.'

Katie looked at the dark shadows under Robbie's eyes and knew he was not joking. 'What's wrong with you?' said Katie hesitantly. 'Have you got cancer?'

'Leukaemia,' said Robbie. 'I've had the works. Chemo, chemo and more chemo, and last year a bone marrow transplant. And now it's come back – and they told me yesterday that there's no further treatment.'

'So, what now?'

'What now indeed? They said that chemotherapy is "no longer an option." They can give me blood transfusions to keep me feeling better, and to keep the bleeding at bay – but it won't work for ever.'

'What will happen to you?'

'I'm still not quite sure. I think I'll just get weaker and weaker and eventually the bleeding will catch up with me, and that will be that.'

'You mean you'll die?'

'Yes, I mean I'll die.'

Katie looked at Robbie's drawn face: 'How old are you?'

'Twenty-two.'

'You're so *young*.'

'Leukaemia's a young person's disease. At least I've had *some* life. At least I wasn't wiped out as a kid. Poor little devils. They don't know what's hit them. One minute they're playing cops and robbers: bang, bang, you're dead! And the next minute it's for real. Bang, Bang. Their noses bleed and their mouths bleed, and they're covered in bruises and they die. At least I've had *some* good life.'

'Are you angry?' said Katie.

'No, not any more. I've worked through that one. I used to be

66

angry . . . shouted at the priest, shouted at God. But not any more. I'm just sad, I suppose. I don't want to die. I've got so much to do. I want to travel, to write, to make love, get married, have kids. I want to do all the mad dangerous things I've never had the guts to do, and all the dull, boring, ordinary things that normal people do.'

Katie took his hand across the table. 'It's not fair,' she said, 'It's just not fair. How can you bear it?'

'I can't,' said Robbie, and suddenly he was crying like a child.

Katie moved to the seat next to him and took him firmly in her arms, the way she took her own children when they were desolate. She felt his shoulder blades, pitifully thin under his woollen dressing gown and realised with a shock that the processes of disease were already far advanced in him. How long had he got? Did he know? How could one survive with the knowledge of impending annihilation?

Robbie withdrew himself gently from Katie's arms. 'Thanks,' he said, 'I needed that.'

'Be my guest,' said Katie, grinning. 'Sorry I hadn't got the regulation tissues.'

'You've got a comfy shoulder,' said Robbie. 'Feels like people have cried on it before.'

'A few,' said Katie. 'Three kids and sundry lovers. But no one's needed it as badly as you did right then.'

'I believe you.'

'Have you got a girlfriend, Robbie?'

'Not now. I had one when I was at university, a lovely Irish redhead called Siobhan but she went back to Dublin and I went into hospital and that was that. She wrote for a while, but now she's engaged to a lawyer and I can't even pretend that she's mine anymore.'

'No one since Siobhan?'

'No, not really. You see I loved her so much I didn't really want anyone else and anyway, three-weekly chemo for months at a time doesn't leave one a lot of time or energy for courting.'

'And you never made love to her?'

'She was a devout Catholic and she didn't feel free. We did a lot of kissing and such like, but that was all.'

'And now you feel cheated?'

'Yes, I do and it looks as though I'll die without ever having sex and I resent that.'

'I knew a girl once who wrote a poem which began, "Will there be fucking in heaven"?'

'Wonderful! Do you think there will?'

'Sure to be. Wouldn't be heaven without it!'

'Oh, Katie! You've cheered me up no end. You should give the hospital chaplain a lesson on how to speak to the dying!'

Katie thought hard. 'But surely the dying are still real people?' she said.

'Katie, I love you! May I kiss you? There's no one else for miles.'

Katie grinned. 'And I don't care if there is,' she said. 'I should love to be kissed.' Carefully, Robbie put his arms around Katie's shoulders and kissed her on the mouth. Katie put her arms around his waist, and held him gently, her cheek soft against his faint stubble.

'Dear Robbie. I wish I could teach you to make love, but I think that will have to do!'

'I don't think I mind so much now. Who knows who I'll meet up with in heaven.'

'Do you believe in heaven, Robbie?'

'Don't know really. Now the chips are down, the doubts crowd in. I went to church when I was a kid, then gave it up for years. Then, when I got sick, I took it up again. I used to meditate every day and I went on a couple of retreats.'

'Buddhist?' asked Katie.

'No, Jesuit. I'm not a Catholic, but Siobhan got me to see a Jesuit friend of hers when I was first diagnosed with leukaemia.'

'Was he helpful?'

'Yes. Very. He was a bit like you – but not so kissable! No, he was like you in that he was really down to earth. No pious crap, but deadly serious about God and about life. He really helped me.'

'Where is he now?'

'He's gone abroad – just when I most need him. But he's due back next week, so I'll drop him a line: "SOS facing death for real. Come at once." That should bring him!'

'What about your parents. How are they taking it?'

'Badly. Very badly. They can't bear to talk about it. They want to take me to America or Europe — anywhere. They can't bring themselves to accept that this is the end of the road.'

'That can't be a lot of help to you.'

'No. It's not. I'm having to be brave and hopeful for their sake when what I really need to do is have a bloody good howl in my mum's arms — not that she's ever been very good at that.'

'Big boys don't cry?'

'That's right. Still upper lip, old chap!'

'Oh Robbie! You can come and cry on my shoulder any day!'

Robbie looked at his watch. 'Hey! It's supper time. They'll wonder where we've got to.'

'Oh, well. We'd better go back.'

'When's your op?'

'Tomorrow.'

'What ward are you on?'

'Nightingale.'

'Shall I come and visit you?'

'That would be lovely. It would do my image no end of good!'

'Right. I shall bring you roses — red roses. And grapes. And chocolates!'

'Wonderful! I shall wear a frilly nightie and we'll scandalize everyone!'

They stood up and Robbie stumbled. 'Damn. I'm getting weaker.'

'Take my hand.' Katie gripped Robbie's hand firmly and they walked slowly together towards the lift.

Debbie was sitting at the desk when Katie walked sheepishly into the ward. 'Sorry,' she said, 'have I missed supper?'

'No, you're just in time. But we wondered what happened to you.'

'Oh, I met a friend,' said Katie, 'and we got talking.'

11

Mary opened her eyes slowly and looked at the unfamiliar ceiling. She tried to turn over but was stopped abruptly by a sharp pain in her side. Panic seized her and she put her hand up to feel the source of the pain but her hand met a soft barrier of bandage and cotton wool. Of course. Now she knew where she was. They'd done it. They'd taken it off. Slowly she raised her right hand to explore. The left breast was there, a familiar landmark, but the right side felt strangely empty, despite its mound of bandages. So it was true. This was really happening. It was not a bad dream, it was real.

Mary closed her eyes and tried to control the panic that welled up in her. She wanted to scream, to give voice to her grief, to her sense of loss and desolation.

'Mary.' the voice was gentle and vaguely familiar. 'Mary. Open your eyes.' Mary opened her eyes and looked up to see Debbie's face. 'Hello Mary. It's all over. You're back in the ward. How do you feel?'

Mary tried to speak but her mouth was dry. 'Thirsty,' she said at last. 'Sore.'

'Have a little sip of water.' Debbie put her hand behind Mary's head and raised her up enough to drink from the glass and straw she held in her other hand.

She sipped greedily and the water was like nectar in her dry throat.

'Well done. Now, Mary, we're just going to give you a little wash, and put you in a clean nightie and then you'll feel much better.'

Mary surrendered herself to their gentle ministrations and feminine patter and felt strangely comforted. These women were kind and they knew what they were doing. They would look after her. It would be all right. Eventually, they had finished and she lay exhausted between the crisp clean sheets. She closed her eyes and sleep overtook her once more.

The next time she woke it was to see John's anxious face above her. He bent and kissed her gently on the cheek.

'Mary, my darling. Are you all right?'

Mary gazed at him with frightened eyes. She gripped his hand and her eyes filled with tears.

John looked at her with enormous tenderness. 'Mary,' he said gently, but firmly. 'It had to go. It was sick. But *you're* the same and I love you as I've always loved you. Do you understand?'

'Oh John, I love you too. You'll never leave me, will you? Promise you'll never leave me?'

'Mary, Mary.' John was distressed now. 'Why should I leave you. You're my wife, my sweetheart, my life. How could I leave you? I love you *so* much.'

Mary smiled weakly. 'Hold my hand' she said. John took her hand in his and began to stroke it gently. Mary closed her eyes with a faint smile and went back to sleep.

The next time she woke it was to see Tony Giles and Debbie standing at the foot of her bed. Tony smiled at her. 'Ah,' he said, 'so you're awake after all.' He came alongside the bed and sat down on the wooden arm of the chair beside her. 'It all went very well,' he said. 'We got it all away.'

'All of it?'

'Yes, all of it. There were some glands in your armpit, so we had to take those away too. You'll be a bit sore for a few days.'

Glands, thought Mary. What does he mean, glands? She thought about asking but she was too sleepy, so she just nodded.

'Well done,' said Tony. 'You're doing just fine. Now I want you to rest quietly for the next couple of days and I'll be in again on Monday.'

Mary smiled. 'Thank you,' she said. She felt a strange warmth towards this kind gentle surgeon. He would look after her. She'd be all right.

Back in the office Tony faced Debbie. 'That's a nasty one, Debbie. I'm afraid she won't do well. Poor lady. There were three or four big glands in the axilla.'

Debbie looked very solemn. 'Poor Mary,' she said. 'She's *so* frightened. It's almost as though she knows how bad things are, though I don't see how she could.'

71

'I know what you mean. It's spooky isn't it? It's as though she's got an intuition, a sixth sense that she's doomed.'

'Will you refer her to the oncologists?'

'Yes. I've spoken to Dr Radcliffe already. They'll give her radiotherapy and chemo as well.'

'How long will that give her?'

'Lord knows. A year, 18 months, if she's lucky.'

A few days later, at the weekly meeting of the pathologists and oncologists, Dr Andrew Radcliffe took a sip of his coffee while the pathologist fiddled with his slides. Eight-thirty in the morning was not a good time for him, but he'd got used, over the years, to force his unwilling brain into gear. 'Carlisle,' said the pathologist.

Andrew picked up his notes. 'Got it,' he said. 'Mrs Mary Carlisle, aged 40. Carcinoma of the right breast. It's a short history. Large mass with diffuse infiltration. Four large glands in the axilla.'

'Yes, That figures.' Dr Bill Nichol, senior pathologist at the Royal Vic spoke with quiet authority. 'This is a very nasty tumour, poorly differentiated. If you look at the cells in this section of the slide you'll see that the nuclei are large and that there are frequent mitoses. And here . . .' he paused for a moment, 'we have one of the axillary glands. You can see that the normal glandular tissue is nearly completely replaced by tumour. What do you reckon, Andy?'

'Bad news,' said Andrew. 'We'll give her radiotherapy to the chest wall which will hopefully prevent local recurrence.'

'What about chemo?'

'Sure. If we're lucky we may get an 18 month remission, but you never know.'

'It's a nasty disease.'

'You can say that again. Who's next?'

'Roberts. Katie.'

'Oh yes. This is a gynae one. Katie Roberts, 29, stage one cervix. Had a Wertheim's hysterectomy last Monday.'

'Right. This is a happier one. No disease outside the cervix. All the glands are clear.'

'Just as well – she's got three kids and no husband.'

Bill Nichol thought of his own grandchildren and grinned. 'She must be a tough one,' he said.

'Don't know. Haven't met her,' said Andy. 'I'll see her in the next joint clinic. She should do well, though.'

'Right, gentlemen and ladies, that's it for today.' The oncologists gathered up their notes and went their separate ways.

Katie lay in bed recovering from her exertions. Who would have thought a bed bath would leave you absolutely knackered. Yesterday was almost a complete blur. She had a vague memory of being given an injection and a tablet, and then, no more. If yesterday was Monday, she thought, today must be Tuesday. Her vague musings were interrupted by a rather giggly Debbie who came into the four-bed bay bearing a large bunch of red roses. Katie stared enviously. Mary's husband must really love her. Red roses indeed!

'They're for you, Katie! Aren't they lovely?' Debbie was clearly delighted at Katie's good fortune. 'Someone must think you're pretty special.'

Katie took the roses from Debbie in disbelief. She picked up the little envelope – yes, they were indeed for her. Miss Katie Roberts. Who on earth . . . Of course, Robbie! Katie's heart swelled and she opened the envelope. 'For Katie with love from Robbie. Get well soon. I need you.' Katie's eyes filled with tears. Dear Robbie. Two days had passed. How was he? Was he still standing by that window in the corridor, or had he gone home to his parent's house? Would she ever see him again?

Mary looked across at Katie and saw that she was crying. 'Are you all right, Katie?' Her voice was anxious. Katie was the strong one. Katie didn't cry. Katie looked up from the note and smiled. 'I'm fine. Don't worry. Just exhausted. How are you?'

Mary smiled. 'I'm also fine,' she said. 'I saw Tessa this morning while you were asleep. She just popped in to see how I was. She's wonderful. She seems to pass some of her strength on to me so that I feel that I will be able to cope after all.'

Katie smiled. 'I'm glad,' she said. 'Oh, Mary, please forgive me, I must have a little nap.' Katie turned over with care and pulled the sheet high over her shoulders and, thus screened from Mary and the rest of the world closed her eyes and thought of Robbie.

Robbie sat up in his bed and faced the doctors with as much bravado as he could muster.

'How do you feel, Robbie?' Dr O'Neill's Irish voice was gentle.

'So, so. Not very strong.'

'What's his haemoglobin, Anna?'

'Eight point five.' Anna was a tall, thin girl with dark rings under even darker brown eyes. She was struggling to balance her time between her job, studying for her exams and making love to her boyfriend who was a registrar on the surgical firm.

'Right. Four units please Anna, for tomorrow, and then Robbie can go home the following day if he feels up to it.'

'Yes, Dr O'Neill.' Anna made a note in her little black book and hoped that Robbie's veins were better than those of the last young leukaemic she had had to transfuse.

'All right Robbie? I'll come back and see you at the end of the ward round.'

Robbie nodded. 'Okay, Dr O'Neill,' he said with a cheerfulness he did not feel.

'Mary.' Mary woke with a jump from her afternoon nap to find Debbie standing at the foot of her bed with a tall fair-headed doctor in his mid-fifties. 'This is Dr Radcliffe, Mary, from the Oncology Unit.'

'Hello, Mrs Carlisle.' Andy Radcliffe's voice was gentle. 'I'm sorry to disturb you. Mr Giles asked me to come to see if any ray treatment would help you.'

Mary shrank back into the pillows. 'But I thought they'd taken it all away?' she said anxiously.

The tall man smiled, 'How would it be if I were to examine you first, and then we can talk about things and I'll try to answer any questions you may have.' Mary nodded, her throat contracting in panic.

'Nurse, could we have the curtains round, please?' Debbie moved swiftly to draw them and stood quietly at Mary's shoulder.

'May I sit here?'

Mary nodded and Andy sat easily on the edge of the bed.

'When did you discover that you had a breast lump?'

'About three or four weeks ago.'

'And you went to see your doctor?'

'Yes, and he arranged an appointment for me at the hospital and . . . and.'

Andy smiled. 'You saw Mr Dalton first, I think, then Mr Giles?'

Mary smiled gratefully. 'That's right, and here I am.'

'So – it's all been pretty quick, hasn't it?'

Mary nodded. 'Very quick.'

'It must have come as a shock?'

Mary fought back the tears which still came so readily. 'Yes,' she said, 'I still can't really believe it's happened.'

'It does take a while. I think we all believe that cancer is something which happens to other people.'

Mary smiled again, feeling more at ease with this quiet man.

'How have you been since the operation? Is it still very sore?'

'It's much better now, thanks. They've told me the stitches are due out in a few days.' Andy looked enquiringly up at Debbie. 'How's the wound, nurse?'

'Fine,' said Debbie. 'Healing well.'

'May I have a look?'

Mary nodded. 'Shall I take my nightie off?'

'Would that be all right?'

Doctor and nurse together helped Mary to ease her night-gown over the wound, now covered with a light dressing. Andy's examination was gentle but seemed more searching than any Mary had had before. His long fingers probed her neck and over her collar-bones searching for glands involved in the cancer. Sure enough, he found one, a hard mass deep behind her right collar-bone. 'Could you lie down now, please, while I lay a hand on your tummy?'

When his examination was complete Andy and Debbie helped Mary back into her nightie and the doctor sat once more on the bed. He looked thoughtfully at Mary and said, 'How much do you understand about your illness, Mrs Carlisle?'

Mary took a minute or two to answer. 'I know it's cancer,' she said slowly, 'and Mr Giles has told me he's taken it all away.'

Andy sat thoughtfully for a moment. How often he had heard the surgeons declare that they had 'taken it all away.' How difficult this issue of truth telling was. What *should* one tell a terrified woman whose disease was disseminated at diagnosis. Should one tell her the real unvarnished truth: that she had a particularly

75

aggressive tumour which had already spread to the glands in her armpit and her neck, and that short of a miracle she would be dead in less than two years? Some people, a few, would want to know the full truth, but this lady was clinging desperately to hope and it would shatter her to know what he really thought.

Slowly, he began the familiar patter, near enough to the truth for his patient at this precise moment. After all, who could know what would happen. Statistics are one thing, but each patient is an individual and breast cancer is an odd disease. Sometimes the people one expected to do well went downhill despite all treatment whilst others lived on to confound their carers and prove all prognostications wrong.

'That's right,' he said easily. 'As far as we can see, it's all been taken away. What we are suggesting is that we give you a little ray treatment just in case there are a few stray cells left behind.'

Mary relaxed. This sounded logical. 'Will it hurt?' she asked. 'And what about my hair?'

Andy smiled. 'No,' he said gently. 'I promise you it won't hurt at all. It's really very like having an ordinary X-ray except that you have it every week day for about four weeks. Your hair won't be affected at all but you will feel very tired.'

'And then I'll be all right?'

'We hope you'll be absolutely fine. But we'll want to keep an eye on you so we'll see you regularly in the outpatient clinic to make sure.'

Mary relaxed visibly. 'When does the treatment start?'

'Let's see.' Andy pulled out a battered notebook. 'I think we should give you a couple of weeks to convalesce, and then we'll begin. Why don't we say around the first week in June? We'll send you an appointment.'

Mary nodded. At least she'd have a little breathing space. Andy straightened himself up. 'Goodbye, then, Mrs Carlisle. We'll meet in a couple of weeks.'

Mary smiled shyly. 'Goodbye.'

12

Robbie sat on his bed waiting for Dr O'Neill to return. To his surprise, he felt quite calm. His encounter with Katie had been a watershed, a turning point. True, there might be no future in terms of career or marriage, but she had given him a powerful reason for living. He must live long enough to see Katie through her operation and back on her feet again. She must get well so that she could live life for both of them. He would die, but some of his spirit would live on in Katie. His secret musings were interrupted when Dr O'Neill entered his room and closed the door.

Rory O'Neill was Irish through and through, a gold medal honours graduate from Trinity College, Dublin. Just how he had come to take root so far away from home was a mystery to Rory's friends and enemies alike, and sometimes even to himself. For better or for worse, however, he was settled now, head of a large haematology unit at the age of 36. Rory was a good doctor, both clever and conscientious. Most of the time he enjoyed his work, but today he felt grossly ill equipped for the task ahead. The trouble, he knew, was that he was too fond of Robbie. Although Rory didn't realise it, he identified with Robbie McAllistair as a fellow Celt. Somehow, he saw himself in this bright young man, and his sense of failure was the more acute.

What on earth could he say to Robbie that would not destroy his hope? During the two years that he had been ill, Robbie had demanded total honesty from his carers. He had made it very clear from the outset that it was *his* body which was sick, and he wished to know exactly what was happening to him and how the doctors proposed to treat his illness. In some ways, this had made things easier for both of them: Rory enjoyed teaching and he taught Robbie about leukaemia and its treatment. It had been both moving and exciting when they'd found a marrow donor and it seemed there had been a real chance of a cure.

Now, all this was over. The disease had recurred despite all his treatment and now it was simply a matter of time before things got out of hand. Rory cursed what he saw as his own weakness. Professor McFarlane, his mentor from Edinburgh, would have taken this in his stride. Just a few oblique words about having a rest from treatment for a few months, and Robbie would have been satisfied, and gone away with his hopes intact. The Professor would not have understood Rory's personal 'involvement' with his patients.

'You can't afford to get too close to your patients, my boy,' he had said. 'Treat them kindly, but let them know that you're in charge and that you make the decisions.'

Well, old Alex McFarlane was dead now, and there was a new generation of doctors and, more important still, a new generation of patients, young men like Robbie McAllistair who demanded, politely but firmly, to know what was happening to them and exactly why such and such a line of treatment was being recommended. They would arrive bearing newspaper cuttings about the latest experimental anti-cancer drugs and ask why these were not being used on them.

Well, now the moment of truth had come, and he must explain to Robbie once more that there was no mileage in giving him more chemotherapy and that he would die quite soon. Rory felt sick and anxious. He hated emotional scenes of any description and this was bound to be emotional. He feared that he might cry himself and thus risk losing Robbie's respect. He who had for two years been Robbie's hero and protector must now reveal that he also was human, that he had lost his power as Medicine Man, that he was only another human being.

Rory sat down on the edge of Robbie's bed. 'Well, Robbie,' he said. 'How are you?'

Robbie thought for a moment. 'Tired,' he said. 'Weak, and getting weaker.'

'You'll feel better after the blood transfusion.'

Robbie fiddled with the bed cover. 'I know,' he said. 'But for how long?'

'It depends.' Rory was cautious.

'On what?' Robbie's question was sharp and Rory knew there was no evading it.

'How your white cells behave. What happens to your platelets.'

'How long have I got?' At last he dared to ask it. *The* question.

'I don't know, Robbie.' Rory was guarded.

'But you can guess.'

'Yes,' said the doctor, 'but I could be wrong, and that might not be helpful.'

Robbie was silent for a while. Then he said softly, 'I need to know. I have things to do before I die.'

Rory said nothing.

Robbie looked Rory full in the face. 'Dr O'Neill,' he said, 'you've always been straight with me and I'm grateful for that. I know you can't cure me. I know I'm going to die. I'm asking you to tell me how long *you* think I'm going to live, so that I can work out what to do. Surely that's not an unreasonable request? You know I won't hold it against you if you get it wrong.'

Rory looked thoughtful. 'All right Robbie,' he said gently. 'You're not going to find this easy. My guess is that you've got about four to six weeks.'

Robbie winced and his eyes filled with tears. 'I hadn't . . .' his voice was strained, 'I hadn't realised that it would be quite . . . quite so soon.'

Rory sighed. 'I'm sorry,' he said. 'You *did* ask.'

'It's fine,' said Robbie. 'I told you, I need to know. I have things to do.'

Rory looked puzzled. 'What sort of things, Robbie? Would you like to tell me about it?'

Robbie was quiet for a moment. Then he said shyly, 'Well, I've met someone, a woman, another patient and I'd like a little time to get to know her.'

Rory smiled. 'Robbie,' he said, 'I'll keep you going as long as I possibly can. We'll make a bargain. You must tell me when you've had enough, when life is no longer worth living. Okay?'

Robbie smiled. 'It's a deal,' he said. 'Thank you.'

Rory stood up. 'We'll transfuse you tomorrow,' he said, 'and see how you feel. Right?'

Robbie grinned. 'Right,' he said.

'Katie, you've got a visitor.' Katie looked up at the sound of the nurse's voice and saw Robbie standing diffidently outside the ward. She sat up and a shy smile transformed her face. 'Hello,' she said. 'How are you?'

'Fine,' said Robbie. 'Just fine. Can't you see how pink I am? I've had five pints of blood.'

'You look great,' said Katie grinning. 'Almost as red as my roses!'

'So, they arrived?'

'The day before yesterday. I felt like a film star. You are kind.'

'My pleasure.' Robbie smiled and fell silent, not knowing quite what to say.

Mary laid down her book and got up from her chair. 'I think I'll go for a little walk,' she said. 'John should be here soon.'

Katie smiled gratefully. 'Robbie,' she said, 'this is Mary, my room mate. We keep each other going.'

'Hello, Robbie,' said Mary. 'It's good to meet you. Now, I must be going.'

After shaking Robbie's hand, Mary moved off leaving Katie and Robbie on their own. Robbie drew his chair closer to the bed. 'How are you?' he said. 'Tell me the truth.'

Katie grimaced. 'Lousy,' she said. 'I'm sore and I'm full of wind and I can't go to the loo!'

'Was it a very big op?'

'Pretty big, as far as I can gather. They don't just take out the womb but they clear away all the glands that might be involved with tumour, and any other bits and pieces.'

'Do they think they've got it all away?' said Robbie, trying to sound casual.

'They say they have.'

'Do you believe them?'

'I don't know,' said Katie. 'No. I think I do. I don't think Dr Townsend would lie to me.'

'Is he the consultant?'

'Chauvinist!' Katie laughed. 'It's a *she*! Liz Townsend. She's the registrar. Australian. Quite a lady.'

'Sounds great. And you trust her?'

'Yes.'

'So, that's good news. I knew you'd be okay. You've got to be!'

'How come?'

'We can't *both* die, can we?' he said urgently. 'You're going to live for both of us.'

Katie reached over and took Robbie's hand. 'Bring your chair closer,' she said. 'I need a cuddle.'

Robbie dragged his chair as close to the bed as it would go and then standing up took Katie in his arms. Suddenly, it was Katie's turn to cry. She buried her face on Robbie's chest and sobbed gently, feeling his arms strong around her. Robbie buried his face in her hair and kissed the top of her head gently.

After a minute or two Katie detached herself gently. 'Damn,' she said. 'Can you pass me a tissue?'

Robbie passed her a tissue and sat there quietly.

Katie blew her nose hard. 'Sorry,' she said. 'Don't know where that came from!' Robbie took her hand and squeezed it. 'Dear Katie,' he said. 'I wish I could stay and look after you.'

'It's not fair,' she said. 'It's just not fair. Why does it have to be you?'

'Hey, Katie! This gets us nowhere. You know there's no answer to the *why me* question.'

'I know there's no answer. But that doesn't mean I can't ask it!'

Robbie smiled. 'Touché,' he said.

'What does your guru say?' Katie was clearly not satisfied.

Rory sighed. 'My Jesuit guru? Same as me – there *is* no answer. That's how things are.'

'Have you heard from him?'

'No. Not yet. I phoned a couple of days ago and left a message on his ansaphone. I think he's due back today.'

'Will he come and see you?'

'I don't know. He might, if I can't get to him.'

'He sounds pretty special,' said Katie.

'He is.' Robbie's voice was warm. 'I'd like you to meet him.'

'I'd like that too,' said Katie.

'How long do you think you'll be in?'

'About another week or so, I expect. And you?'

'It depends.'

'On what?' said Katie.

'On you!' said Robbie, grinning.

'How do you mean, on me?'

'Well, Dr O'Neill said I could stay till I felt ready to go. He knows my parents are very anxious and he understands that I need some space while I face up to the future. And, well, I told him there was someone special in the hospital that I wanted to get to know . . .'

'So, he's letting you stay?' said Katie, amazed.

'Well, yes,' said Robbie. 'He explained that they're happy to bend the rules a bit for people like me.'

'Are you saying you're staying in hospital to be near me?' Katie could not believe her ears.

'You've got it!'

'Robbie, you're impossible!'

'Why?' said Robbie calmly. 'I love you!'

'But you've only just met me!' said Katie in delighted disbelief.

'I haven't got time to hang about,' said Robbie quietly.

Katie held out her arms, and Robbie stood up once more and held her tightly. Once more, Robbie buried his face in her hair, oblivious of the sound of soft steps.

Debbie's voice broke the silence. 'Excuse me,' she said awkwardly. 'I'm sorry to interrupt, but are you Robbie McAllistair?'

Robbie looked up and reluctantly let go of Katie. 'Yes,' he said. 'What is it?'

'There's a phone call for you at the nurses' station. 'A Father David Meredith. Shall I put it through to Sister's office so you can be private?'

'Oh please,' said Robbie gratefully, 'that would be really kind. How did he find me here?'

'He rang your ward, and Sister knew you were coming up here, so she transferred the call.' Debbie smiled, delighted to see Katie with a friend.

'Great,' Robbie turned to face Katie. 'It's my guru,' he said excitedly. 'He's home! I'll be back in a minute.'

Katie watched Robbie's back disappearing down the corridor and felt her heart turn over. She had not felt such a tenderness for years, nor had her heart ever before been full of such a strange mixture of joy and grief. But then she had never before met anyone quite like Robbie and she had never before found herself loving a man under sentence of death.

Her musings were interrupted by the return of a smiling Robbie. 'He's coming tomorrow, Katie!' he said. 'He's got some friends locally and he'll stay a few days and see me every day. I've told him about you and he's looking forward to meeting you.'

Katie smiled at his excitement, wondering that anyone could be so pleased at the thought of seeing a priest. Her own experience of clergy people had been confined to the weddings and christenings of some of her friends. She herself had never been able to persuade her lovers to visit a register office, let alone a church. She'd always steered clear of priests, sure that they would disapprove of her and her way of life. She voiced her fears to Robbie: 'But Robbie, will he want to meet me? Aren't I, well, a "fallen woman"? After all, I've got three illegitimate children!'

'Katie Roberts, be quiet! The only thing you've fallen into is bad luck. Do you really think a friend of mine would reject you because you're not married? You must have a pretty poor idea of the clergy? Anyway, David is not like your regular clergyman, he's special. Now, I must go back to the ward or they'll think I've run away. How would you like to fall into my arms just once more?' Katie grinned. 'I guess I fall easy,' she said and held out her arms towards him.

13

David Meredith's expression was grave as he replaced the telephone on its receiver. So, it had come. The moment that Robbie had so feared was upon him. He had no doubt that he must go to him at once. The fact that his bags were as yet unpacked and his mail unopened now seemed unimportant – they could wait. Robbie could not. He looked in his address book for Susie Wellington's number, and dialled rapidly. 'Susie? Hello. It's David,' he said. 'Yes, I'm back. Look, can you give me a bed for a few nights? There's someone I need to see in the Royal Vic. Right. Thanks. I'll be with you around six tomorrow. Thanks. Bye.'

David sat down at his desk and lit a cigarette. He leafed through his diary: no major commitments till next week. For once he had been strict with himself about leaving space to unwind after a trip abroad. Well, the unwinding would have to wait, or rather it would happen anyway, while he drove and while he drank Ben and Susie's good red wine.

Poor Robbie. Life had been very cruel to him, and now this: facing death in his early twenties. Yet, he'd sounded positively cheerful over the phone, a little 'high' perhaps, but somehow peaceful as well. It was amazing how that young man had grown over the last couple of years. He was a very different Robbie to the immature lad Siobhan had introduced him to one evening in Oxford. His thoughts turned briefly to Siobhan. Lucky for her she hadn't married Robbie, or now he'd have two desolate young people to comfort and counsel. Stubbing out his cigarette just before it burned his fingers, he turned to his pile of mail and started the task of opening, reading and sorting.

It was around three o'clock in the afternoon the following day when David's battered Ford drew into the car park at the Royal Victoria Hospital. He had been more than usually pensive during the four hour drive, Robbie never far from his thoughts. Although he knew from experience that it was useless to plan what he was going to say to anyone, his mind kept returning to the inevitable question of the dying: 'Why me?' and 'What is the meaning of my life?' And then, of course the ultimate mystery: 'What happens when I die?'

David had 'accompanied' dying people before but never one as young as Robbie. Well might this young man demand of God 'Why me? What have I done to deserve this?' His, David's, role here would be to remind Robbie that he must feel free to ask these questions, that he, like Job, had a right to demand of his maker 'Why pick on me?' Just what the answer would be, he could not tell. Perhaps Robbie would hear only the echo of his own anguished voice, or, perhaps, the answer would come in that mysterious 'still small voice' of which the prophet spoke (1 Kings 19), the voice that left a legacy of peaceful certainty. Or, perhaps God would roar at him out of the whirlwind, as he did at Job, overpower him with an awesome presence, fill him with such a sense of wonder that his questions seemed no longer relevant (Job 38).

David lit another cigarette and sat quietly in the car as he smoked, trying to still his mind and heart so that he might be fully open to Robbie and to the God in whom they both believed. Faith for David was a dark affair, sometimes quite painful, occasionally utterly mind-blowing. He had long since let go of the idol of a beneficent Santa Claus God to whom Christians had a private hotline, and lived more or less at ease with the concept of a God of paradox, a God who was totally 'other', mysterious, transcendent yet somehow personal, loving and intimate.

A three year spell in the East had given him a deep respect for the other great religions, and whilst he was clear that his own roots were deeply planted in Christianity, in Catholicism and in the Society of Jesus, (the Jesuits) he had many friends of other faiths and in other Christian Churches. He meditated with Buddhists, celebrated the Passover meal with Jews and worked closely with his many Anglican and Protestant friends.

So, he thought, what do I bring to Robbie? How would *my* faith stand up to the possibility of imminent death? Do *I* believe in the 'Four Last Things'?[1] Do *I* believe that Robbie is soon to stand before the throne of God to be judged, and then be consigned to heaven or hell for all eternity? David Meredith inhaled

---

[1] The Four Last Things are Death, Judgement, Heaven and Hell.

deeply on the remnants of his cigarette and tried to summon up his own 'credo'. I *do* believe in God, he thought, whatever she or he is like, and I believe that God is loving, that I am loved, and that Robbie is loved, in all our foolishness and vulnerability. Do I believe that Robbie could go to hell, he asked himself, and he knew that he did not. Thirty years of working with all conditions of men and women had left him convinced that the majority of people are more wounded than sinful, more trapped by their unconscious drives and their environment than actively wicked. Even the most despised of society, the perverts and the child-abusers were a sad and wounded people, so often terribly sinned against in their youth, so that they seemed doomed to follow the same sad and shameful path as their abusers.

But, if I don't believe in hell, David thought, do I believe in heaven? And what about reincarnation? What happens to the spirit of a man or woman when he or she dies? Is it extinguished like a candle? Does it pass into 'another being?' Does it go to be 'united with God', and if so, what on earth does 'united with God' mean? O Lord, he thought. We were all brought up to accept these pious phrases, and we never stop to question what they mean. I don't know, he thought. I don't know anything.

Yet, I *do* believe there is a loving God, and I *do* believe that the spirit lives on after death, and what's more I believe that Robbie, when he dies will be somehow more whole, more happy, more vibrant and more fully himself than he has ever been before. I don't *know* anything, he repeated to himself, but I believe, I *really believe* that death is the beginning, not the end. Having thus prepared himself he looked to left and right to see that he was not observed, threw his cigarette butt on the ground and set off for the main entrance of the hospital.

Robbie was asleep when David arrived so the priest had a chance to watch him unobserved. He was shocked at the change in him. Robbie had clearly lost a lot of weight and there were dark shadows under his eyes. His long hands lay thin and still on the bed and David's heart turned over as he realised that this was how those familiar hands would look in the stillness of death. Damn! he thought. It's not fair. Here am I, fit and well at 57, and this boy won't even make it to Christmas. He could understand a little how a parent must feel, how they would offer to trade their own lives for those of their children. Robbie stirred uneasily in his sleep, and David longed to hold him in his arms like the son he'd never had. There would be time enough for that, he thought. Luckily, he was in no hurry, and lowering his gaunt six foot two into the chair by the bed, settled placidly down to wait.

It was nearly half an hour before Robbie woke, opening his eyes to find his friend and mentor in the chair beside him. 'Hello,' he said, delightedly, 'how long have *you* been there?'

David grinned. 'Oh, a couple of hours,' he said.

Robbie sat up, now wide awake. 'It never ceases to amaze me,' he said, 'how the clergy can be such outrageous liars!' Swinging his legs over the edge of the bed he held out a hand. 'Thanks for coming. It means a lot to me.'

David took the thin hand in his, and as Robbie stood, pulled the young man into his arms in a great bear hug. For a moment Robbie clung to him, and let the tears fall unashamedly down his face and on to David's shoulder. David held him gently. 'It's all right Robbie,' he said, 'let it out. Let it out.'

At last, Robbie's tears were spent and he climbed back on to the bed. David looked at him, his eyes full of compassion. 'I'm sorry I was away,' he said. 'You've had a rough time.'

Robbie took a deep breath. 'It's strange,' he said. 'Most of the time I'm pretty good, quite calm really. I think I've come to terms with dying, at least as much as anyone can, but accepting it doesn't stop it hurting.'

'It never does.' David's voice was gentle.

'The sadness comes in waves – it catches me out when I'm least expecting it, especially when people are being nice to me!'

'How are your parents taking it?' said David.

'Hard. They can't accept it really. They have to go on pretending it'll all be fine, that I'll have a spontaneous remission or that a cure will be discovered in the nick of time.'

'That can't be very helpful.'

'It isn't,' said Robbie succinctly.

'I'm sorry,' said David quietly. 'You must feel very much alone.'

'I do,' said Robbie, then corrected himself. 'No, that's not true, I did, but now things have changed a bit.'

'Oh?' David was surprised.

'I've found a friend. A girl called Katie.'

David's eyebrows went up a fraction. 'Tell me about her,' he said with a smile.

'She's a patient here,' said Robbie, 'on the gynae ward. She's got cancer of the cervix and she's just had a hysterectomy. I met her last week, the night before her op. She suddenly appeared out of nowhere when I was standing by a window in the corridor thinking about throwing myself out.'

David felt an icy hand grip his heart, but he said nothing. Robbie continued. 'We got talking, really talking, no barriers, no small talk . . . It's been amazing. I've never met anyone like her.'

'How old is she?' said David.

'Twenty-nine,' said Robbie, conscious for the first time of the seven-year gap between himself and Katie.

'Is she married?' said David, wondering what was coming next.

'No,' said Robbie, calmly. 'But she's got three kids.'

David mentally anchored his eyebrows in their normal place. 'That must be quite a handful,' he said.

'It is,' said Robbie seriously. 'The eldest, Emma, is 13 and especially difficult.'

'Who's looking after the children?' said David.

'A girlfriend of Katie's is staying there for a few weeks.'

'Does she have a partner?'

'She did,' said Robbie, 'but he walked out when he found out she had cancer.'

'And you Robbie?' said David gently, 'How do you feel towards her?'

Robbie was silent for a moment, looking down at his hands. When he spoke it was slowly and uncertainly. 'It probably sounds crazy,' he said, 'but I feel incredibly tender and protective towards her. I want desperately for her to be happy, for life to be good to her. From what she's told me, it seems she's had such a lousy deal so far. She was abused as a child, left home in her teens to get away from her stepfather, and then had to leave her partner because he was violent. Now Katie's just discovered that he abused her daughter Emma when she was a small child.'

David listened intently. 'Go on,' he said quietly.

'That's it really. I love her. It's as simple as that. It's not quite the same as falling in love, but I just know that I love her and want to look after her.'

David smiled. 'She must be very special, Robbie,' he said warmly. 'When am I going to be allowed to meet her?'

'Tonight if you like.'

'Fine. I'd like that.'

Robbie paused for a moment. 'How long have we got?'

'Today?' he said. 'I have to be at Susie's around eight.'

'I meant this week. How long can you stay? There's so much I need to talk about.'

'Don't worry. I knew there would be. We've got a week. Will that be enough?'

Robbie grinned. 'That should be enough,' he said, 'even for me! Just so long as you give me a phone number so I can contact you if I get in a panic.'

'Of course,' said David calmly. 'Did you think I wouldn't?'

'No. Will you be able to come again . . . when I'm . . . when the time comes?'

David fought to keep back the tears. 'Robbie: you have only to say, and if I possibly can, I'll come.'

Katie was sitting up in bed reading a magazine when Robbie and David arrived. She looked up at the two men – Robbie with a broad smile on his face and beside him, a tall thin somewhat older man.

'Hello, Katie,' said Robbie, 'I've brought David Meredith to see you.'

David smiled and took Katie's shyly proffered hand 'Hello, Katie. Robbie's been telling me about you.'

Katie grinned. She liked the look of this man in the shabby anorak and corduroy trousers, so very different from what she had expected. 'Did he tell you how we're scandalising the hospital by kissing in public places?' she said. Robbie laughed delightedly. This was his Katie, the irrepressible, the forthright. He had been afraid that she would be on her best behaviour with David but he need not have worried. Katie, the unchurched, had no preconceived ideas about what was or was not 'proper' conversation with the clergy. She received David in her own inimitable way, treating him as the human being that he was.

David grinned. 'Robbie and I have had a little hug too,' he said, 'just to confuse the onlookers.'

'Robbie needs lots of hugs,' said Katie spiritedly. 'They ought to be prescribed by the doctors!'

'What about you Katie?' asked David. 'How are you feeling?'

Katie became serious again. 'Do you want the polite answer or the truth?'

'Tell him the truth, Katie,' said Robbie. 'Anyway, you couldn't be polite if you tried!'

'Okay,' said Katie. 'You asked for it! I feel awful. I've got pains in my stomach, and I still can't go to the loo, and I don't feel like eating and I've got a sore tail. Apart from that, I'm fine!'

David grinned. 'I shall go and look in my little black book,' he said, 'for a prayer for the bowels! Bless, O Lord, this thy constipated servant and grant him, stroke, her, a mighty deliverance from his, stroke, her, distress.'

Katie and Robbie collapsed in giggles. 'I bet that does more good than senna,' gasped Robbie, 'and without giving you the gripes.'

Suddenly Katie stiffened. 'I think your prayer is working already,' she whispered. 'Can you go and find me a nurse Robbie?'

'Goodbye Katie,' said David hurriedly, 'I'll come and say hello again tomorrow, if I may.'

'That would be lovely,' said Katie, 'but for God's sake, go now before I lose any more of my dignity!'

Debbie arrived panting and David and Robbie took their leave with a brief 'Good luck, Katie' and a wave.

It was nearly half past seven by the time David arrived at Ben and Susie's house. Susie led him into the kitchen where she was cooking supper and sat him down at the kitchen table with a mug of coffee. 'You look bushed,' she said. 'What have you been up to?'

'I'm only just back from South Africa,' he said, 'preaching, giving a retreat, visiting people.'

'How was it?'

'Exciting. Moving. Humbling. Exhausting . . . I need time to process it all'

'So, tell me more about what brings you here.' said Susie.

'This young friend of mine is in the Royal Vic,' said David, 'he has leukaemia and we thought he'd got it beat, but now its recurred and they say there's nothing more they can do.'

'Oh, Lord,' said Susie. 'What about a bone marrow transplant?'

David shook his head. 'He had one last year,' he said. 'Went to hell and back with the chemo and the isolation[2] and now its all for nothing.'

'That's a hard one.' Susie's voice was gentle. 'Hard for him and hard for you. . . . Oh, but what the hell can you find to say to him?' She was getting angry now. 'Tell him Jesus loves him?'

'I think he knows that already,' said David quietly. 'You're in a cynical mood tonight, Susie. What's up?'

'Oh, nothing really. I need a holiday,' said Susie, a little ashamed of her outburst.

'How's Ben?' said David, mentally setting Robbie and his grief on one side.

'He's fine. His usual placid self. He's nearly finished his latest book, an abstruse treatise on some twelfth-century Cistercian monastery.'

David grinned, 'Sounds riveting!'

Susie laughed. 'Now who's being cynical!' she said.

'How are the kids?'

'They're great,' said Susie with a smile. 'Martha's 14 now, and madly in love. I can never get her off the phone these days. You were lucky to get through! And Charlie's having a ball at university.'

'What's he reading?'

'Psychology, of course. What did you expect!'

'Ah . . . lots of good clean fun with rats and mice and mazes and things.'

'That's about the price of it,' said Susie. 'Tell me more about your lad, if it's not breaking confidentiality.'

'I'd like to. It's quite a sticky one and you might be able to help, keep me posted about how he is. Would that be a possibility?'

---

[2] Patients undergoing bone marrow transplant are treated with powerful drugs which destroy the cancer cells and also damage the immune system and they have to be nursed in a special germ-free environment. This means that they are in cubicles and have very few visitors. This is renowned for being a very traumatic experience.

'I should think so, if he wants it and his doctors are happy. What's the story?'

When David had finished Susie gave a low whistle. 'Wow,' she said. 'That's quite a story. How does the woman feel about him? It's putting a lot on her.'

'I know, but they seem very comfortable with each other. Like a couple of kids almost.'

'It feels like one of those crazy holiday romances.'

'Or a wartime love affair,' said David.

'That's it. You've hit the nail on the head, David. Perhaps it isn't so strange after all. *He* goes to the front line to be killed knowing he's loved and *she* has the memory to keep her warm on the long lonely nights.'

'He's deadly serious about it,' said David. 'He's determined not to die until she's back on her feet after the operation and until she knows that she's loveable.'

'What did you say her name was?' said Susie curiously.

'I didn't, but it's Katie. Katie Roberts. Why do you ask?'

'It rings a bell. The story, I mean, that's all.' She gave the sauce an extra stir and then turned round from the Aga. 'Isn't there a bolshie teenage daughter as well?'

'That's right. Emma,' said David. 'What a very small world this is, Susie.'

'What do you want me to do?' Susie moved imperceptibly into professional mode.

'Nothing, at the moment,' said David. 'Thanks for hearing me out. Talking about it was helpful. I'll know more what they need when I've spent some time with them both.'

'How do you deal with the God-stuff?' asked Susie suddenly. 'I can't handle that. I just get so damn angry at the cruelty of it all, the out and out injustice.'

'Oh come on, Susie,' said David. 'Life's like that. You know that as well as I do. You don't believe in a God who inflicts pain and disease on innocent young people any more than I do. The difference between us is that I believe in a God who is somehow caught up in the anguish of it all, while you think that's all pious nonsense.'

'Okay, okay,' said Susie, 'lets call a truce. I just wanted to know what you'd *say* to him. I wasn't baiting you – it was a serious question.'

'There's no set patter. Like you, I respond to what people say – it's an intuitive process as much as anything. I can't tell you what I'm *going* to say, but tomorrow night I'll tell you what I *did* say. Okay?'

'Okay, Father!' Susie's voice was light-hearted again. 'How about a glass of wine? Supper's just about ready.'

David grinned. 'I thought you were never going to ask me! Shall I set the table?'

14

David and Robbie sat comfortably together in silence on a large rock overlooking the valley. The sun was warm on their backs and the river wound its silver way several hundred feet below. 'God, it's beautiful,' Robbie exclaimed. 'I can't bear to think this is probably the last time I'll see it.'

'We can come back tomorrow, if you like,' said David quietly.

'You know what I mean, David. What I'm saying is that I'm not ready to go. I'm too young. There are sights I need to see, things I need to do. I want to go back to Venice in February and walk in the fog. I want to climb Kilimanjaro, to see the great wall of China. I want to make love to Katie.'

David was silent, sensing that Robbie's remarks were rhetorical, cries of rage and longing. At last he spoke. 'Are you scared, Robbie?' he said gently.

'Scared?' said Robbie.

'Yes,' said David. 'Scared of dying.'

'No,' he paused. 'Yes. Of course *I'm* scared,' said Robbie. 'Everyone's scared of the *process* of dying. I'm scared of bleeding to death, of tasting the blood in my mouth again, of having my nose packed and half choking on the blood trickling down the back of my throat.'

David felt the icy hand on his heart again and his throat contracted. Slowly, with infinite precision, he rolled a cigarette, lit it and then, after taking a long hard draw, said quietly, 'Where is God in all this for you, Robbie?'

Robbie was silent for what seemed a long time, and then said, 'I think he's up to his neck in the shit beside me. I have this sense of his being around, but impotent to help me. I keep thinking that he ought to be able to rescue me but he seems powerless. But I know he's there, most of the time anyway.'

'Does this sense of his presence comfort you at all?' asked David, marvelling at his young friend's faith.

'Sometimes,' said Robbie slowly. 'Not all the time. Sometimes I think he's just as scared as I am. We're neither of us very brave.'

94

'I think you've got a wrong idea of what it means to be brave, Robbie,' said David. 'Courage is more about enduring than about escaping. Sometimes we're trapped and there's no way out and the only thing to do is to hang on with bleeding finger nails. I think you're facing death in much the same way that Jesus faced it, by bearing the pain and the fear as best you can. Inevitably, because you're human, you fall under the cross. But like him you get up and stumble on again. There *is* no easy way.'

Robbie was crying now. 'But David, what's the *use* of it all? It's not as if I'm dying *for* someone. Nobody benefits from my suffering. It's all such a bloody waste. Why? Why? What's the *use* of it all?'

David put his arm around Robbie's shoulder and the young man leaned against him. At last, the weeping ceased and Robbie straightened himself up.

'Thanks,' said Robbie. 'I needed that.' He blew his nose and they sat in silence for a while. Then Robbie spoke: 'How do *you* see it, David? What do *you* think is going on?'

'With God you mean?' The priest's eyes were focused upon the cigarette he was rolling.

'Yes,' said Robbie.

David took a deep breath. 'I don't know, Robbie. I honestly don't know . . . but I can tell you what I believe, if that would help.'

'Yes, please,' said Robbie. 'I think it would.'

'Well, let's begin at the beginning.' David crossed his fingers, praying that the right words would come. 'I believe in God – a wild mysterious God, the God we get a glimpse of in the encounter of Moses on Mount Sinai. Like the Jews, I believe in Yahweh, the all powerful creator God who is both *transcendent*, out there, beyond all the knowing, and yet is also *immanent*, in our world, as close, as the Muslims say, as the neck of your camel. I believe that this God made the world, made you, made me, and that he or she is somehow involved in an ongoing process of creation. I don't believe in what some people call "the watchmaker God", that is in a God who made the world, wound it up and then left it to its own devices. As I said, I believe that God is still creating the world, labouring as St Paul puts it, like a woman giving birth.'

'Are you saying that God controls everything that happens?' asked Robbie. 'That he *gave* me leukaemia?'

David was swift to answer this one. 'No, Robbie,' he said. 'I don't think that. You see this is where it gets so muddly, so mysterious, illogical if you like. I believe that God created the world to be as it is – wild and beautiful, flawed and dangerous. Violence and disease are part of the world which we have been given. That's the way things are. I don't believe that God intervenes in the natural processes of the world. He doesn't *cause* earthquakes, nor does he prevent them. They happen. The earth's crust is unstable. That's just the way things are.'

Robbie nodded. 'I'm with you so far,' he said, 'but I still can't grasp the idea of God as an ongoing creator if you say he isn't making things happen.'

David sighed. 'It's difficult, Robbie. I don't know that I can explain it any better. I think to grasp it you have to take into account the incarnation, the fact that God took on human nature and came to live amongst us. It was Jesus the man who, as the son of God was born and lived in Palestine two thousand years ago and it's Jesus the Christ, the second person of the Trinity who is alive and active, suffering yet glorious, in our world.'

Robbie frowned. 'I still don't understand.'

'I'm sorry Robbie,' said David apologetically. 'I think the only thing you can do is look at your own experience. You said yourself that you had the sense of God as being *in* your suffering.'

'Yes,' said Robbie. 'I'm quite clear on that.'

'I think all you can do is try to hold those two things together,' said David, 'your lived experience of God-with-you and the impossible theology of Christ in the world.'

'It works for you?' asked Robbie.

'Yes, Robbie,' said the priest gently, 'it works for me.'

'Where do *you* meet God, David?' Robbie asked quietly.

'Everywhere, Robbie,' said David smiling. 'Absolutely everywhere. In the world – the sea, the stars, the wind, the flowers. And in people, in you, in Katie, in everyone. I meet him particularly in the events of every day. In the events of my life, in all my relationships.'

'And you *know* God loves you?' Robbie was still puzzled.

'Yes, Robbie,' said David quietly. 'I am very sure that I am loved, just as I am sure that *you* are loved.'

'I wish I had your certainty,' said Robbie.

'I think that certainty is a gift, Robbie,' said David. 'It comes and goes. I think you are going through the dark valley at the moment and your doubt is part of that experience.'

'What do you mean "the dark valley"?' asked Robbie.

'It's an Old Testament image,' said David. 'Think of the 23rd psalm: Though I walk in the Valley of the Shadow of Death, no evil will I fear.'

'You are there, with your crook and your staff . . .' Robbie remembered the comforting words.

'That's right,' said David. 'As I said earlier, you just have to hang on with bleeding finger nails or rather you have to believe that you will be *held*. Do you remember that poem of Helder Camara's that I read you when we first met, when you were first diagnosed as having leukaemia?'

'You mean "Go Down"?' said Robbie.

'That's it,' said David and began to recite the words of the diminutive Archbishop of Olinda and Recife in Brazil's turbulent North East.

> Go down
> into the plans of God.
> Go down
> deep as you may.
> Fear not
> for your fragility
> under that weight of water.
> Fear not
> for life or limb
> sharks attack savagely.
> Fear not the power
> of treacherous currents under the sea.
> Simply, do not be afraid.
> Let go. You will be led
> like a child whose mother
> holds him to her bosom
> and against all comers is his shelter.

'You've got an amazing memory!' said Robbie. 'For poetry, yes. But not for names!' said David wryly.

'Where can I find that?' asked Robbie.

'It's in a little book called *The Desert is Fertile*,' he said, 'but I'll write it out for you.'

'Thanks,' said Robbie gratefully. 'I think it's what I need, right now.'

'I thought it might be.'

'He's right though. Sharks *do* attack savagely, and I feel as though I'm being carried down a river by a mighty current and any minute I'm going to be sucked under or go over a waterfall.' Robbie was near to tears again. 'I'm sorry, I wish I was braver.'

David felt near to tears himself. 'You *are* brave Robbie,' he said. 'Don't think you're not. But you're a human being, and it is a human characteristic to fear death. We *all* fear it. That's why we need someone to walk alongside us, insofar as that is possible.'

'What am I going to do when you've gone?' Robbie's voice was strained.

'You'll be all right,' said David with a confidence he did not really feel. 'You'll see. Anyway, I'm not going yet.'

'Hold my hand, David,' said Robbie suddenly. 'I'm so afraid.'

David held the thin hand between his own two strong ones, and bowed his head.

Several minutes passed, and Robbie said, 'Thanks. I'm okay now. It's just that the fear comes in the most terrifying waves and I get completely paralysed.'

'I know,' said David quietly, letting go the hand.

'Were you praying?' asked Robbie shyly.

'Yes,' said David. 'Were you?'

'Sort of.' Robbie's voice was uncertain.

'Are you able to pray at the moment?'

'It's hard. Terribly hard, but I try.'

'In what way is it hard?' said David softly.

'I suppose I don't know what to say,' said Robbie slowly. 'I don't know what to pray for. My instinct is to scream at God to cure me, but somehow that doesn't feel right.'

'Feel right?'

'I have a sense that the time has come to accept what is happening to me, to say "yes" to God, not "no".'

David was silent for a short while. 'That's easier said than done, isn't it?' he said. 'That's what Jesus experienced in the Garden of Gethsemane.'

'I suppose it was,' said Robbie slowly. 'I hadn't thought of it like that.'

'I think you must feel okay to think of it like that if it helps.' David's voice was full of tenderness. 'What you are going through is very similar to Jesus' experience and there's a sense in which he's experiencing it with you. That's why you are aware of his presence. You are there in Gethsemane *with* him, struggling to accept the cup.'

Robbie was very quiet. 'I wish *you* could be there with me,' he whispered.

'I wish I could too,' said David. 'But I can only be a bystander, a frightened spectator. My turn will come, no doubt.'

David rolled a cigarette and they sat quietly together for a while. It was Robbie who broke the silence. 'David.'

'Yes,' said David, turning to face his young friend.

'Do you believe in Heaven and Hell?' Robbie asked tentatively.

'Heaven, yes,' said David firmly. He paused. 'I'm not so sure about hell.'

'Will I go to heaven, do you think?' Robbie's voice was fragile and David longed to take him in his arms like a child. Instead, he said firmly, 'Robbie, I'm quite sure you will.'

'I wish I was as confident as you,' said the young man.

'Is there something you're worried about, Robbie?' The priest and counsellor in David was suddenly alert to the possibility of guilt.

'Sort of,' said Robbie quietly.

'Do you want to tell me about it?' David sat quietly, relaxed and focused.

'I'm not sure,' said Robbie. 'It's something that happened a long time ago.'

'It's your decision, Robbie,' said David gently. 'I can't make that one for you.'

Robbie paused, and then he said quietly, 'I think I'd like to tell you. But it's pretty awful.'

'Take your time.' David was all priest now.

'It happened when I was at school,' said Robbie slowly, 'in my last year. When I was 17. There was a younger boy, a very beautiful boy, called Crispian.'

David said nothing.

'He had a crush on me, I was his hero: a prefect, captain of the first eleven and so on.'

'And you,' said David quietly, 'what did you feel about *him*?'

'At first, nothing much. I was amused, a little irritated by his devotion.'

David was silent. How often he had listened to variations on this theme. 'But that changed?' he said.

'Yes,' said Robbie. 'One day I had to supervise a group of junior boys swimming, and Crispian was among them. It was the first time I'd seen him undressed. His body was *so* beautiful. He was slim and his skin was pale, like milk, like ivory. I found myself watching him in the shower, watching him move about naked. I thought he wouldn't notice, but suddenly he turned and caught my eye, but he was so innocent I could see that he didn't know what I was thinking.'

David's heart was heavy. Partly because he guessed what was to come but mainly because of the way the British boarding school system exposed vulnerable young men and boys to the temptation to explore their burgeoning sexuality in ways that they were bound to regret.

Robbie looked up at him. 'Are you shocked?' he asked.

'No, no Robbie,' said David. 'Just thinking. Go on.'

'Well, that night he came to my study to borrow a history book. I asked him if he'd like some cocoa, and he accepted. And then, and then . . .' Robbie looked at the floor.

David said nothing.

'I, I told him to take off his clothes.' Robbie stopped, unable to continue.

David's heart ached for the young man in his shame. 'And you had sex with him?' he said very quietly.

Robbie's voice was barely audible. 'Yes,' he said.

'He was willing?' asked David.

'No,' said Robbie, 'but he was scared and desperate to please me.' The tears coursed down the young man's face.

'How long did this go on for?'

'All through that term,' said Robbie. 'I told people I was helping him with his history prep, and he came to my study every evening and,' Robbie could hardly speak, 'and I used him.'

'How did it end?' David's voice was infinitely compassionate.

'When we came back after the Christmas holidays, I sent for him and assumed he'd go on, but he'd changed.' Robbie felt sick with shame.

'Changed?' said David.

'Yes,' said Robbie. 'He was still scared of me, but he said he didn't want to do it any more. He said,' Robbie stumbled over his words. 'He said it made him feel dirty.'

'What did *you* say?'

Robbie paused, 'I was angry and a bit scared too that he'd rat on me,' he said. 'I told him that if he told anyone I'd tell the Head that I'd caught him with another boy and that they'd be sure to believe me rather than him.'

'What did he say?'

'Nothing, he just stood there looking at me.' Robbie buried his head in his hands for a moment and then he began again. 'When I'd finished he began to cry. He cried and cried and I got angry with him and just pushed him out of my study.'

Suddenly, Robbie himself was crying openly, terrible harsh sobs quite unlike his previous quiet weeping. 'Sometimes, sometimes,' he gulped, 'I wonder if this illness could be God punishing me . . .'

David pulled out his tobacco. 'Shall we treat this as confession, Robbie?' he said.

Robbie nodded. 'Please.'

'Fine.' said David softly. 'Just sit there for a moment and try to lay the whole sorry business before God.'

Robbie sat with his head bowed while David rolled a cigarette. Then, laying the unlit cigarette beside him on the rock, the priest too bowed his head. Eventually, he spoke. 'Robbie,' he said, 'what you did was very wrong, a gross abuse of your power over a younger boy. He trusted you and you betrayed that trust.' The priest paused and looked at Robbie, but the boy's head was bowed. 'But,' he continued, 'it is not uncommon for adolescent boys to explore their sexuality in this way. The tragedy was that you were not mature enough to control your own lust and that Crispian didn't have the strength to refuse you. If he had done, you would probably both have got over it.'

Robbie was silent, his face drawn and white. David looked at him with a deep compassion. 'I think you were a very thoughtless, selfish and immature young man caught up in a torment of adolescent lust, but I do not think you *intended* to hurt Crispian and I am quite sure you had no desire to harm him. Am I right?'

Robbie nodded miserably.

'Well, Robbie, if *I* can forgive you, how much more readily will God? He will just gather you into his arms and hold you tight.'

Robbie was silent.

'Do you believe me?' David looked into Robbie's tear-stained face.

Robbie turned again, the tears coursing freely down his cheeks.

'Good. Now, tell God of your sorrow and your shame and I will, as his priest, give you his forgiveness.'

When the sacrament had been completed, priest and penitent sat in silence for some time. Eventually, it was Robbie who broke the silence.

'David.'

'Yes, Robbie.'

'What about Crispian? Do you think I could have injured him, I mean psychologically?'

David thought for a moment, then said very quietly, 'I suppose it's possible.'

Robbie was silent for a while but when he next spoke his voice was much stronger. 'What do you think I should do, David? Should I write to him, and say I'm sorry.'

'Would you like to do that, Robbie?'

'Yes. I really would.'

David smiled. 'I think that would be a good thing to do then. Do you know his address?'

'No, but if I write to the school they'll find him.' He paused a moment. 'Would you give him the letter, David, when I'm gone? Tell him how sorry I am.'

David's heart turned over. The spectre of death seemed suddenly very close.

'I'll be happy to do that, Robbie,' he said quietly.

Robbie was exhausted by the time he and David arrived back at the ward. Sister, who was sitting at her desk looked up as the two men entered.

'Hello,' she said. 'Had a good drive?'

'Lovely, thanks,' said Robbie. 'We went up into the hills overlooking the valley. The sun was really warm.'

Sister smiled. 'I'm glad,' she said. 'I hope you haven't done too much. You look really tired.'

Robbie grinned. 'No,' he said. 'I'm fine. But I might have a little nap all the same.'

David sat on the edge of the bed while Robbie lay back on his pillows. 'Are you okay?' he asked quietly.

'Yes,' Robbie smiled and grasped his hand. 'You can't imagine how much better I feel. It's as though a great weight has been lifted from my shoulders. I feel as though I could run and jump.'

David smiled. 'I should have a good rest first,' he said. 'I'll see you tomorrow.'

15

Susie looked up from her book as David entered the kitchen. 'Hi!' she said. 'Coffee?'

'Yes please.'

'It's on the Aga. I've just made a pot.'

David sat down at the table opposite her and cradled the mug in his hands.

'Well? How was it?'

'We went out for a drive – up into the hills and sat for ages looking down on the valley. It was good.'

'How was Robbie?'

'He was okay. He's sad and frightened, just as you would expect. We talked about dying, and faith and God.'

'And?'

'There was some unfinished business, something from his school days which had been weighing on him. I was able to free him from some of that.'

'Poor kid,' said Susie. 'Your church lays heavy burdens of guilt on its children.'

'Sometimes,' said David. 'This was something a bit different. Anyway, I think its sorted now.'

They sat for a few minutes in companionable silence, then Susie said, 'What are you going to do tomorrow, David?'

'It depends how Robbie feels,' said David. 'It may be that we've done most of the heavy talking today. I rather hope he can have some fun during the next few days.'

Robbie was up and dressed when David arrived at 11 on what was to be their last day together before David went back to his work.

'Hello,' said David. 'You're looking bright today. Did you sleep well?'

'Wonderfully,' said Robbie. 'I feel really good.'

'I'm glad. What would you like to do today?'

'Could we have a picnic by the river?' said Robbie. 'It's such a lovely day. And – could Katie come too?'

David smiled. 'Of course she can,' he said. 'Is she up to it?'

'I've been and asked her and she'd love to. She's getting dressed.'

'Grand. Shall we go and collect her then?'

Di Ashton, the ward sister, smiled at Dr O'Neill as Robbie and David walked out together. 'How's that for a priest?' she said.

'That's never a priest,' said Rory.

'It is so,' said Sister grinning broadly, 'and a Jesuit to boot! He's a friend of Robbie's. He's taking him out for a picnic.'

'Great!' said Rory. 'Just what Robbie needs. I don't think he's got long to go.'

'Poor lad,' said Di. 'Are you planning to keep him in till he dies? He seems very happy here at the moment. Those parents are *so* anxious and over protective. I think he'd go mad if he went home with them in their present state.'

'That's what I figured,' said Rory. 'I've told him he can stay until he feels ready to go home. I think we owe him that, don't you, Di?'

'Robbie can stay as long as he likes as far as I'm concerned,' she said. 'So long as he's happy I think we're doing something for him. It must be hellish just waiting for things to go wrong again. How long do you think he's got?'

'I told him four to six weeks, but looking at the way his blood counts are going, I think it will be a lot shorter than that.'

'What do you think will happen?'

'He'll bleed,' said Rory quietly. 'His platelets are falling every day.'

'Will you give him a transfusion?'

'I'll cross that bridge when I get to it,' said Rory. 'He's got a girlfriend, a patient in the hospital, and I promised to keep him going as long as I could.'

'A girlfriend?' said Di surprised.

'Well, a friend, anyway,' said Rory.

'Ah, so that's why he keeps popping off to Nightingale Ward. Well I never! Good luck to him.'

David lay back on the grass with his eyes closed, listening to the murmur of the stream and the sounds of laughter from where

Robbie and Katie sat together under a tree. What an amazing gift their friendship was; no matter that their happiness was doomed to be cut short. People could live whole lifetimes in a few days, love and know their love returned in a brief encounter. The two had sat in the back of the car holding hands as he drove along the winding road that led to the place they had chosen for a picnic. They talked incessantly, quite unabashed by his presence. Katie was clearly much better. She told him that his prayer for the constipated should be bottled, or rather printed and distributed free on the NHS. It had solved all her problems.

All, it seemed, was well at home. Emma was being as good as gold and helping to look after the two younger children. Katie herself would be going home in a few days. The pathology results were back and the surgeon had assured her that the tumour had been completely removed. Mary had gone home that morning, still anxious, but thankful that her operation was safely over.

Robbie laughed and squeezed Katie's hand. 'It sounds as though you're all set,' he said. 'You don't really need me any more.'

'Don't tempt fate you stupid boy,' Katie retorted. 'Anyway I haven't finished with *you* yet. There are things you have to learn before you go, and I propose to be your teacher.' David's eyebrows rose a fraction. Well! He thought. Robbie hadn't mentioned that one! Time would tell.

Now, lunch was over and they were all relaxing in the sunshine. Seeing Katie and Robbie becoming even more closely intertwined, David decided it was time he went for a walk. He called out to them. 'I need some exercise. See you in an hour or so?'

'Sure. We'll be fine.'

Robbie lay back on the grass and pulled Katie down beside him. 'How about my first lesson?' he said.

'Shame on you, Robbie McAllistair,' said Katie laughing, 'and me only 10 days post op!'

Robbie sat up beside her. 'Katie,' he said urgently. 'I may not have very long.'

Katie's eyes filled with tears. 'I was only teasing,' she said, and undoing her blouse, pulled him close to her. 'Hold me Robbie,' she whispered. 'Hold me tight.'

They were both asleep when David returned, lying like the

babes in the wood in each others arms. Katie's hair was dishevelled and her blouse untucked from her skirt. David smiled and withdrew to a discreet distance and pulled out his tobacco.

David let himself quietly into Susie's house and found her dozing on the lawn in a deck chair.

'Hello,' she said. 'You're back early.'

He grinned. 'I've got my children in the car. Could you bear to give them tea?'

Susie pulled her maternal bulk out of the chair. '*Both* of them?' she exclaimed. 'What fun! Bring them in.'

Robbie and Katie were strangely subdued as the four of them had tea on the lawn. Katie smiled. 'You two look exhausted,' she said. 'Why don't you have a nap on the lawn before David takes you back to school?'

Robbie looked at Katie and she grinned. 'That would be lovely,' she said.

'We had a nap after lunch, but after all, we *are* convalescent!'

Susie went into the house and returned with a large brown blanket and two pillows. 'I'm afraid I've only got one blanket,' she said, 'so you'll have to share!'

Robbie grinned mischievously. 'I think we'll manage,' he said.

'I suggest you take yourselves off to the end of the garden,' said Susie, 'and then David and I won't disturb you with our chatter. David, why don't you carry the bedding and get them settled and I'll refill the teapot.'

'Well!' said Susie, when David returned.

'Well, indeed!' said David, and they sat in contented silence, drinking their tea.

It was close on seven when Susie looked at her watch. 'Hadn't you better take them back, or would you like me to give them supper?'

'Susie, would you?' said David. 'They'll have missed hospital supper and I can't bear to take them back just yet, it's such a lovely evening.'

'Sure. No problem. I'll make some spaghetti. You'd better go and wake them or they'll be getting a chill with the dew.'

David found his two charges talking quietly together.

'Hello,' said Robbie. 'Come and join us.'

'We're invited to supper,' said David. 'Would you like that?'

Katie's eyes lit up. 'That would be wonderful,' she said. 'Isn't this a beautiful place.'

'And isn't Susie wonderful,' said Robbie. 'What an amazing lady. What does she do?'

'She's a psychotherapist,' said David. 'We're very old friends.'

'How did you meet her,' asked Robbie.

'Ah, it's a long story,' said David. 'I was at university doing post graduate work and she helped me over a difficult patch. Then we became friends. I always stay with her and Ben when I come here.'

'She's such a *comfortable* lady,' said Katie. 'She makes you feel safe.'

'She'll like that!' said David. 'Now, shall we go into supper?'

Susie had set the table with a cloth and candles with a small bowl of roses in the centre. Katie was entranced. She had never been inside a house like this before, let alone dined by candlelight. 'Oh!' she exclaimed, 'isn't it pretty! Thank you so much.'

Susie smiled. 'Would you like to come upstairs and wash your hands, Katie?' she said. 'The men can use the downstairs cloakroom.'

Katie followed Susie up the wide stairs and into a large untidy bedroom containing a double bed with a faded but still beautiful patchwork quilt. 'The bathroom's through there,' said Susie. 'I'll join you in a moment.'

Again, Katie marvelled at the beautiful carpeted bathroom and compared it wryly with her own cramped one with its always overflowing basket of the children's dirty washing. As she washed her hands in the basin with its old fashioned brass taps Katie looked at her face in the mirror. There was the beginnings of a faint tan over her hospital pallor, and her eyes were sparkling. What an amazing day. She thought about it as she tried unsuccessfully to comb her wild hair with her fingers.

She emerged into the bedroom to find Susie running a comb through her thick black hair. 'Do you want to borrow my hair-brush, Katie?' she said without turning round. 'Your hair's almost as bad as mine. Here, have a go at the mirror.'

As Katie sat at the mirror doing her hair, Susie sat comfortably on the bed behind her. 'Has it been a good day, Katie? For both of you?'

Katie smiled at Susie's reflection. 'Oh yes,' she said. 'It's been wonderful. We know it can't last, so we're determined not to waste a single minute. He's *so* brave,' she said, 'and he's so loving. I've never met anyone like him in my life. It seems so cruel that we didn't meet before.'

Susie nodded. 'Life is very cruel sometimes,' she said. 'One can only be grateful for the good moments, cherish love whenever it is given. This is a love which will stay with you for ever, whatever the future holds. And you're giving Robbie something infinitely precious, something which makes it possible for him to live these last weeks and days to the full.'

Katie stood up from the dressing table and turned to face Susie. 'You're very kind,' she said. 'I wish you were my mum! Maybe my life would have been different if you had been.'

Susie heaved herself off her bed and took Katie in her arms. 'Let me be your mum for today,' she said, and gave her a mighty hug. Katie clung to her briefly, and as she let go, Susie said, 'Well, daughter, we'd better go and feed our menfolk!' Hand in hand, the two women walked down the stairs.

16

'Joe, dear. Have you *been*?' Jeannie Peterson enquired of her husband. Joe sighed. Damn the woman. She always knew. Did she listen at the bathroom keyhole or something, or weigh the toilet paper?'

'No,' he said shortly. 'I expect I'll go later.'

'But Joe,' said Jeannie plaintively, 'you always go in the morning.' Joe rustled his newspaper and then said in a tired voice. 'Not always I don't, Jeannie. Not these days, anyway.'

His wife was silent for a few minutes and Joe breathed a sigh of relief. For a while they were quiet. Joe reading his paper while his wife cleared away the breakfast things. After a few minutes she began again, more tentatively. 'You didn't go yesterday, either, did you Joe?'

Joe remained silent, apparently lost in his paper. After a while, his wife began again. 'Joe . . .'

This time her voice was strained and Joe, sighing audibly, put down his paper. 'Jeannie,' he said, 'you know I hate talking about this sort of thing. I wish you'd just leave me alone! I'm sure it'll right itself soon enough. I'll try to take a bit more exercise. That'll sort it out.'

His wife was silent and he saw her eyes fill with tears. Joe rose slowly to his feet and put his arm around the old woman's diminutive shoulders. 'Jeannie, lass, what is it?' he said tenderly, 'What's the matter? It's not like you to cry?' Jeannie buried her face on Joe's chest and let the tears flow. He held her firmly but she felt his ribs beneath his shirt in a way she had never done before. Joe smoothed her hair and then bending kissed the top of her head. Then, with his arm still around her, he led her to her chair, and lowered her tenderly into it. Pulling his own chair alongside hers, he put his hand over hers and repeated his question.

Jeannie fumbled for her handkerchief and blew her nose fiercely. 'I'm sorry, Joe,' she said, 'I know I'm being stupid, but I'm so worried about you.'

'Worried about me?' said Joe, exasperated. 'Just because I'm a bit constipated? Oh Jeannie!'

'It's not just that Joe,' she said. 'You know it isn't. You've changed so. You've lost weight, and you're so pale and tired. Please, please Joe, won't you go to the doctor?'

'Eee lass,' said Joe, with his rich Yorkshire accent, 'the doctors are so busy these days. I'll go to the chemist tomorrow and get some senna pods. That'll put me right.'

It was dark when the pains began. Joe cursed silently to himself and, swinging his legs over the side of the bed, fumbled for his slippers. Downstairs, he filled the kettle and sat down to wait for it to boil. What the hell was wrong with him, he thought? It must have been something he'd eaten. He replayed the previous day's meals, in search of a reason for his indisposition but the truth was, he'd eaten very little. They'd had soup and bread and butter for supper and only a sandwich for lunch. He didn't seem so hungry these days, in fact he really only ate to placate Jeannie, to keep her from going on at him. The kettle boiled and Joe began to pour it into the mug containing the bicarbonate of soda.

It was then that the pain really hit him, overwhelming him like a tidal wave so that he dropped the kettle and sank to the kitchen floor with a moan.

Jeannie Peterson stirred in her sleep and then woke. Automatically she reached across to feel for Joe, but her exploring hand met no familiar warm resistance. She relaxed. Joe must have gone to the toilet. She'd better leave him be. He wouldn't like her knocking on the bathroom door and asking if he was all right. Still sleepy, she smiled to herself. Even after 50 years of married life he was still a very private sort of man. I suppose we both are, she thought, remembering their wedding night when she had been too shy to take her nightie off.

He'd been so gentle with her, so kind, and just held her in his arms so that she could get used to the feel of having a man so close to her. It had been a long time before she could relax enough for him to make love to her and to tell the truth she'd never really enjoyed it, always been a bit embarrassed by the whole business. Perhaps that was why they'd never had children. Well, those days were long since gone. It would have been nice to have had children, she mused, but it had just never happened and neither she nor Joe had wanted to have any tests. Children were a gift from God, she'd always said. Not a right. It was a shame, though, because Joe would have loved a son, and he'd have been a wonderful father.

Jeannie lay there, quietly pondering as the minutes passed, waiting for Joe to come back to bed. She looked at the clock on the table beside her bed – a quarter past three. Joe was taking his time. Suddenly, she began to worry. I'll give him another five minutes, she thought, then I'm going to see if he's all right.

To her surprise, Jeannie found the bathroom in darkness, then assuming that her husband had gone downstairs to use the lavatory, she made her way slowly down the stairs. It was only then that she heard it – a faint moaning sound coming from the direction of the kitchen. Jeannie's heart turned over. Joe! He must be in trouble. Why hadn't he called her? She felt cold with fear.

Once on the ground floor Jeannie moved more surely. She hated the stairs and had more than once suggested to Joe that they sell the house and move into a nice modern bungalow. After all, now that they were both in their eighties they had to think practically about the future.

As she entered the kitchen, Jeannie's heart began to beat chaotically and she felt sick and dizzy. Joe lay on the floor with his eyes closed, his face pale and his breathing laboured.

'Joe! Joe!' Jeannie knelt down by her husband and touched his face. He opened his eyes and Jeannie could have wept with relief. With an enormous effort, Jeannie pulled herself together, and taking a cushion from one of the kitchen chairs, she put it under her husband's head.

Once by the phone, Jeannie realised that she had left her glasses upstairs. Tearing the list of phone numbers off the notice board, she held it away from her face, but still the numbers were only a blur. Fighting the panic that threatened to overwhelm her, Jeannie grabbed the receiver, and, thanking God for the large digit phone Joe had bought last winter, dialled 999.

Bill Jenkins of Ambulance Control listened patiently until the old lady stopped talking. 'All right love,' he said kindly. 'I've got the address: 25, Alexander Road. We'll be with you in a few minutes. Now, have you got a blanket handy?'

Jeannie gulped, comforted by Bill's kind, authoritative manner. 'They're upstairs,' she said, 'and . . . and I'm not very good on my legs.'

Bill took a deep breath. Mustn't hassle the old lady, or she'll fall downstairs and then there'll be two of them. 'How about an overcoat?' he suggested gently, 'or a towel. Anything to keep him from getting too cold.'

Jeannie arranged two coats over Joe's prostrate form. 'Oh God, let him be all right,' she prayed. 'Please let him be all right. Don't take him away from me. Not yet. Please. Not yet.'

The doorbell rang sharply and Jeannie rose painfully from where she was kneeling beside Joe. Thank God. At last, they were here.

'Mr Wilson, the Casualty Officer's on the phone, will you take it, or shall I get him to leave a message?'

Miles Wilson groaned to himself. It was going to be one of those nights. He looked up at the anaesthetist. 'Okay if I leave Mandy to close up?' he said. 'She's quite a nifty seamstress.'

Donald Acres smiled at the young doctor. 'Sure,' he said.

Mandy Fellowes beamed with pleasure at the compliments and, turning towards the scrub nurse, said, 'Three O silk please,' in as nonchalant a voice as she could muster.

The scrub nurse, who was more than a little in love with Mr Wilson and was not pleased to see him go, said nothing as she ripped open the suture packet with a practised hand and clipped the small curved cutting needle securely into the needle holders.

'Nice and neat now, Miss Fellowes,' said Donald, 'after all, she's going to want to wear her bikini again.'

Mandy grinned but said nothing. Then, plucking up courage, turned to the scrub nurse and said, 'Have you got a finer pair of forceps please, these seem a bit clumsy to me.' The scrub nurse scowled, but she knew that she would gain nothing by arguing. Taking a small parcel labelled 'Mr Wilson's forceps' she ripped the covering off and handed the instrument to Mandy.

Miles pulled his mask down off his face, and, leaning wearily on the counter in the theatre sister's office, took the phone and said, 'Miles Wilson here. What's the problem?'

'Mr Wilson? It's Tessa McDermot. I'm the new casualty SHO. I've got an old man down here with what looks like a faecal peritonitis.'

'What makes you say that?' Miles voice was crisp. If she was right there was no time to hang about. Elderly men with perforated colons were a very poor risk.

Tessa held her ground. 'He's got a three month history of increasing constipation and weight loss and he collapsed an hour or so ago with acute pain. His belly's rigid and tender and his blood pressure's in his boots. I've put up a drip and ordered four units of blood.'

This girl knew her stuff. Miles' voice was gentler. 'Well done, Tessa, thanks. We'll be right down.' He stuck his head round the theatre door. 'You okay, Mandy?'

Donald answered for her. 'She's doing famously. One knit, one purl. Not a dropped stitch among them.'

Miles grinned. 'Well done, Miss Fellowes,' he said. 'When you've finished, come down to Cas. It looks as though we've got another customer.'

'Mrs Peterson?' Miles looked down at the old woman sitting huddled in the armchair in sister's office and felt absurdly impotent. Why was it he always seemed to be landed with breaking bad news to poor old ladies in the middle of the night? At least Mandy was with him this time. She'd be able to comfort her. Women were better at that sort of thing. 'Mrs Peterson,' his voice was weary. She looked so old, so frail, a bit like his own Gran.

Jeannie looked up. Her eyes were red with crying and fatigue. 'How is he, doctor?' she said. 'He will be all right, won't he? Tell me he's going to be all right.'

Miles was silent for a moment. Then steeling himself he began with the time honoured formula. 'I'm afraid I've got some bad news for you, Mrs Peterson . . .'

Jeannie's eyes were wide with terror. 'He's not . . . he hasn't . . .' her voice trailed off.

Miles looked at her imploring face and then across at Mandy. The young doctor said nothing, her eyes fixed on her hands clasped in her lap. Damn the girl. She wasn't going to be any use to him.

'Mandy,' he said, quietly, 'would you ask Staff Nurse to come in here for a moment please.'

Joanna Driver, the Staff Nurse on night duty on Men's Surgical was a stalwart Yorkshire woman in her late forties. She took one look at Jeannie and, pulling up another chair sat down beside her and put her arm around the old woman's shoulders. She nodded to Miles who began again. 'Mrs Peterson,' he said, trying a different tack, 'I'm afraid your husband's very poorly.'

Joanna tightened her grip around the frail shoulders. How thin she was, poor old thing, like a frightened bird.

Jeannie looked up at the young man before her. How tired he looked, and how young, with his blond hair ruffled and his green theatre trousers under the grubby white coat. What was he trying to tell her? What was wrong with Joe? Miles took another deep breath and began a third time. 'I'm afraid your husband's very poorly, Mrs Peterson. He's got a growth in the large bowel which has perforated and given him a faecal peritonitis. We've done all we can but it wasn't possible to remove the tumour. We've given him a defunctioning colostomy so he'll have to wear a bag. But it'll be touch and go. I'm very sorry.'

Jeannie said nothing. What was there to say? Her mind had gone blank the moment the doctor had said 'bad news'. 'Growth', he'd said. What did he mean, 'a growth?' And peritonitis – wasn't that what you got with appendicitis? Perhaps Joe had appendicitis. She twisted her hanky, sodden with tears, in her hands.

Joanna looked across at the two doctors who sat silent and uncomfortable in front of her. 'Mrs Peterson,' she said gently, 'is there anything you'd like to ask the doctor, or shall I get you a nice cup of tea?' Jeannie looked at her gratefully and nodded.

Miles met Joanna's gaze, and rising thankfully to his feet said, 'Goodbye Mrs Peterson. I'll leave you with nurse now.'

Jeannie looked at him through her tears and tried to thank him but no words came and he disappeared through the door. She sat silently, gripping the sodden handkerchief while her mind tried to focus on the doctor's words. Bad news. Bad news. She'd thought he was trying to tell her that Joe was dead. What did he mean, a colostomy? She struggled to get her thoughts together but she was just too tired and the tears began again.

Joanna stood up quietly and then kneeling on the floor, took the weeping woman gently in her arms. For the first time in these last few terrible hours, Jeannie felt safe. This kind nurse would look after her. She would look after Joe. She wouldn't let him die.

'Mrs Peterson . . .' Joanna's voice was gentle. 'Mrs Peterson, I'm going to get you some tea, and then we'll talk about what the doctors just told you.'

A few minutes later, Jeannie gratefully took the tea from Joanna and raised it to her lips. Her hand shook so much that it spilt on to the saucer and she put it down wearily.

'Mrs Peterson,' said the nurse, 'take the cup with both hands and then you won't spill it. The tea will make you feel better. You've had a terrible night.'

When the old woman had drunk about half the tea, Joanna spoke to her again. 'Mrs Peterson, did you understand what the doctor told you?' Jean shook her head. 'Not really, dear,' she said. 'It was all such a shock. My mind kept going blank.'

'I thought as much,' said Joanna. 'Would you like me to explain things again?'

Jeannie nodded. 'Yes, please,' she said quietly. 'I feel calmer now.'

Joanna smiled. 'It's been a terrible shock, hasn't it?'

Jeannie nodded. 'Yes,' she said. 'You see, I found him lying on the kitchen floor and I just didn't know what had happened.'

'Did you ring the doctor?' Joanna's voice was warm and friendly and Jeannie felt somehow comforted.

'I tried,' she said, 'but I'd left my glasses upstairs, and I couldn't read the numbers.'

'Oh, how awful for you,' said Joanna. 'I'm always losing my glasses and I'm blind as a bat without them.'

By the time she had told the nurse about the kind man in Ambulance Control, the journey in the ambulance and what had happened in Casualty, Jeannie felt strong enough to ask Joanna just what it was that the doctor had said.

Slowly, Joanna explained that Joe's bowel had blocked off because he had cancer and that tonight there had been a leakage

116

of the bowel content into the tummy cavity, causing a severe inflammation called peritonitis. She explained that this was a very serious complication and although they would do everything they possibly could, Joe was very poorly indeed and might not pull through.

This time, Jeannie understood everything she was being told, but it was still hard to take in the information. Part of her wanted to think that this was all a terrible mistake, and that the doctors had somehow confused Joe with some other patient. The other, more rational part of her knew that it was all true. There was a terrible logic about it all; the pieces of the jigsaw, Joe's constipation, his weight loss, his tiredness, all fitted together now. It was as she'd suspected. Joe had cancer. He was a very sick man and . . . Here her thoughts stopped. Time enough to think about that, Jeannie. Listen to the nurse, she's saying something to you.

It was light now. Joanna looked at her watch. Lordy, she thought, it's nearly six. I must get a move on. 'Mrs Peterson,' she said, 'I'll go and phone the Intensive Care Unit and find out if you can see your husband yet.'

She left the room quietly and Jeannie looked around her in bewilderment. She was in some kind of an office. There was a varnished wooden desk and three chairs, a few books and a notice board covered with various bits of paper and a couple of cards. Jeannie ran her hand through her hair. She felt old and tired and very alone.

When Joanna came back she had another, younger, nurse with her. 'This is Polly, Mrs Peterson,' she said. 'She's going to take you to the Intensive Care Unit to see your husband. They'll be keeping him there for a day or so, till he's well enough to come back to the ward.'

Jeannie stood up. 'Goodbye,' she said to the older nurse. 'Thank you for being so kind.'

Joanna smiled and, taking Jeannie's hand said 'Try not to worry, dear, the doctors are very clever these days.'

Polly led Jeannie through what seemed to the old lady to be mile upon mile of bare corridors. There were more people about now, porters and cleaners with mops and giant floor polishing machines. They entered a lift and Polly supported Jeannie's arm as the lift started to move. They were all so kind, Jeannie thought.

117

I could have had a granddaughter like this, if things had been different.

Her reverie was cut short. 'Here we are, Mrs Peterson. This is the Intensive Care Unit.' They went in through the swing doors and Jeannie found herself in a brightly painted anteroom. There were a few leatherette chairs, a coffee table bearing a large ashtray and a bright red door bearing the intimidating notice 'Strictly No Admittance. Please ring the bell for attention'.

Jeannie sat down gratefully, tired after her long walk, while Polly rang the bell and waited, standing, for someone to come.

Soon, the red door opened and a nurse wearing a white tunic and trousers appeared and smiled at Jeannie. 'Hello,' she said, 'you must be Mrs Peterson.'

Jeannie nodded. The nurse laid a gentle hand on her shoulder. 'Your husband's all right,' she said. 'He's clearly a fighter.' She nodded at Polly. 'Thank you nurse. I'll look after Mrs Peterson now.'

Polly smiled. 'Goodbye, Mrs Peterson,' she said, and slipped quietly away.

Lucy Carstairs liked working on the Intensive Care Unit. She was a clever young woman who relished the challenge of working with desperately sick people. She enjoyed the people – contact, too, comforting frightened relatives and listening to the doctors as they puzzled over the complicated array of information which the high-tech machinery produced about their patients. She had just come from one such conversation with Will MacIntosh, the duty registrar. They had debated, too, the ethics of using scarce and expensive resources on an old man with cancer who was doomed to die quite soon, whatever they did.

Now, however, Lucy laid science and ethics on one side and concentrated on putting a frightened old woman at her ease. Leading Jeannie into a cosily furnished interview room, Lucy settled the old lady in an armchair, then sat down beside her. Slowly, she explained that Joe was doing as well as could be expected and that Jeannie could see him in a moment. First of all, however, she needed to warn her that he wasn't round from the anaesthetic yet and that they were helping his breathing with a special machine called a ventilator.

'You'll see all sorts of tubes and wires,' said Lucy, 'but try not to worry. We're just keeping an eye on his heart and lungs and doing a few special blood tests.'

Jeannie nodded, still slightly dazed, and wished that the nurse would stop talking so that she could see Joe.

Lucy smiled. 'I'll take you in now, Mrs Peterson. I'm sorry to go on so but I don't want you to be shocked or frightened by the way your husband looks. Some people find all this hi-tech stuff a bit scary.'

Rising, Lucy took Jeannie's arm and led her gently through the red door and into the ward.

17

Tom Hitchcock opened his eyes and, finding the lights too bright in the Intensive Care Unit, shut them again rapidly, though not fast enough to evade Lucy's eagle eye.

'Hello, Tom,' she said, 'how are you feeling?'

'Bloody awful,' said Tom with his eyes tight shut.

'Tom,' said Lucy firmly, 'open your eyes.'

Tom opened them and scowled.

Lucy grinned. 'Sorry, Tom,' she said, 'but I find it difficult to talk to people when I can't see their eyes.'

Tom grunted.

'Tom,' said Lucy gently, 'why are you hiding?'

Tom's eyes filled with tears. 'Hiding!' he said bitterly. 'There's nowhere to hide in this bloody place.'

'Is that the problem, Tom, that you can't get away from us?'

Anger gave Tom courage. 'It's all very well for you,' said Tom. 'You can get away from *us*, you can go home. But I'm chained to this bloody bed, exposed like a prisoner in the stocks. Sometimes I think I'll go mad.'

'Poor Tom.' Lucy took his hand but he made no response so she withdrew hers. She tried another tack. 'It shouldn't be too much longer, Tom. You're almost well enough to go back to the ward.'

'And you think that'll be better?' said Tom bitterly. 'With a student nurse and the ward cat to look after me?'

Lucy stood up. 'Well, Mr Hitchcock,' she said wearily, 'it seems there's no pleasing you this morning so I'll go and get on with things.'

'Lucy!' His voice was urgent. 'Don't go. Please don't go. I'm sorry to be such a pig – it's just that I feel so low.'

Lucy sat down again. 'It's all right,' she said. 'I just feel so useless. I don't know what to say to help you.'

'Don't worry,' Tom grinned. 'Actually, you help a lot, just by being around, by being you. Don't let's talk about me. Who's the new inmate?'

'Patient to you, Mr Hitchcock!' Lucy was her usual quick-witted self again. 'He's an elderly man in his eighties. I've just been talking to his wife.'

'What's the matter with him?' asked Tom curiously. 'Heart attack?'

'No. Cancer.' Lucy bit her lip. 'Damn,' she said. 'I shouldn't have told you. Forget I told you that.'

'Poor old sod,' said Tom, 'It's no respecter of age is it?'

'No,' said Lucy. 'But it's cruellest in kids. At least he's had his four score and ten.'

'What about me then?' said Tom sharply. 'I'm only 42. I didn't expect to get cancer. What do you think I did to merit losing half my bloody backside?'

'Tom!' Lucy was exasperated. 'I've told you before – you did nothing to *merit* having cancer. It's not a punishment and it's not your fault, it's just b ad luck.'

Tom put out his hand. 'Sorry, Lucy,' he said. 'I didn't mean to go on at you. It's fate I'm angry with, or God, or who ever's up there or out there or wherever.'

'Lucy . . . have you got a moment?' The staff nurse who had appeared at the bottom of Tom's bed was diffident. 'Mrs Peterson asked if she could see you.' Lucy nodded and the nurse disappeared.

She turned to Tom. 'Will you be okay now?' she said gently. 'Has the black cloud lifted a little?'

Tom smiled. 'Lucy, my love,' he said. 'You're like the morning sun dispersing the gloom of night.'

Lucy grinned. 'Get lost,' she said and escaped before Tom could ask her where the hell he could get lost to in such a place.

Mrs Peterson was standing by her husband's bed. She looked tired and very frail. 'I think I'll go now, nurse,' she said. 'I've tried to talk to him but he doesn't seem to know me.'

Lucy looked at Jeannie, standing, waif-like by her unconscious husband. She took the old woman's arm and said, 'Come, Mrs Peterson. Why don't we have a little talk in my office before you go?'

Jeannie turned to look at Joe and Lucy winced at the pain in her eyes. 'Would you like to kiss him goodbye?' she said. 'Maybe that will register with him.' She led Jeannie back to the head of the bed. 'Why not kiss his forehead,' she said, 'then the tubes won't be in the way.'

Tentatively, Jeannie bent over Joe's unconscious figure, and, smoothing his hair, she kissed him lightly on the forehead. Momentarily, his eyelids flickered and Lucy exclaimed in delight, 'Look! I'm sure he knew that was you. My guess is he'll be awake quite soon.'

Jeannie smiled gratefully and Lucy, taking her arm led her towards the office.

Gratefully, Jeannie then sipped the tea which Lucy brought her. She felt she didn't really want to leave this nice nurse and in particular she didn't want to leave Joe.

Lucy smiled at her. 'Who have you got at home Jeannie?' she said.

Jeannie's eyes filled with tears yet again. 'No one,' she said. 'Joe and I never had any children.'

Imperceptibly, Lucy moved further into her professional mode. What was she to do with this frail old lady? She could scarcely push her out on to the street, and yet she could not keep her there. Poor soul, she was going to have to learn to cope on her own.

'How about friends,' she said, 'or a neighbour? Is there anyone who could come and pick you up?'

Jeannie thought for a moment. 'I suppose Jessica might,' she said. 'She's my neighbour. She's a single mum but she's ever so kind.'

'Would you like me to ring her for you?' said Lucy.

Jeannie nodded. 'I'm sorry to be so helpless,' she said. 'It's just that Joe's always done everything and I've always leant on him.'

'Don't worry,' said Lucy. 'It's no trouble. Do you know Jessica's phone number?'

Jeannie shook her head wearily. 'No,' she said.

Before the old lady could apologise Lucy smiled again. 'Never mind,' she said. 'Do you know her address?'

Jeannie felt better. At least she knew something. 'Yes. She lives opposite our house. Number 30 Alexander Road.'

Lucy jotted the address down on a small pad and stood up. 'That should do it,' she said. 'I'll go and ring directory enquiries and see if I can get through to her.'

Jessica Holmes was in the shower when the phone rang. Cursing under her breath she turned off the taps and, grabbing a towel, hurried to the phone wondering who the hell was ringing her at this time on a Saturday morning. 'Is that Miss Holmes?'

'Yes.' Jessica was wary at the unfamiliar professional voice.

Lucy explained that her neighbour had been taken ill and that Jeannie needed help and support. As Jessica listened, her irritation gave way to compassion. Poor old Joe. And poor Jeannie. She *must* be in a stew.

'Of course I'll help,' she said. 'Give me a bit of time to get myself together – about three quarters of an hour?'

Having been assured that that was fine, Jess hung up the phone and returned to the bathroom.

'Who was that Mummy?' Charlotte Holmes called to her mother from her bedroom where she lay sprawled on her bed reading a book.

'It was the hospital. Mr Peterson was taken ill in the night and they've asked me to go and pick up his wife.'

'Poor Mr Peterson. Is he going to die?' Twelve-year-old Charlotte was a kindly child well aware of the facts of life and death.

'I certainly hope not.' Jessica's heart sank at the prospect of a lonely and ageing widow as a neighbour. 'Oh well,' she thought, 'it won't do me any harm.'

'Hurry up, Charlotte,' she said. 'Can you get dressed please? We have to go to the hospital.'

Fifteen minutes later, Jess returned, to find her daughter still buried in her book. Just like her father, thought Jess, oblivious of the rest of the world. She sighed and wondered yet again what their lives would have been like if Oliver had chosen to marry her. Would they have been happy? She had thought so, but he had been so sure that it wouldn't work out. He'd offered to pay for an abortion, but she'd refused angrily, preferring to raise his child on her own rather than wantonly to destroy it. Oliver was married now, to Clarissa, an unspeakably dull ancient historian who, it seemed was barren. How on earth could Oliver love her? thought Jess. Stop it. She spoke sharply to herself and then, without realising it, passed that sharpness on to her daughter.

'Charlotte!' she said. 'Will you put down that book at once and get dressed. We have to go to the hospital and pick up Mrs

Peterson. She's been there for most of the night. The poor thing must be half dead with worry and exhaustion.' Charlotte extracted herself reluctantly from her duvet and wandered round her room in search of her jeans, eventually running them to earth under a pile of discarded sweaters, socks and knickers upon which Michaelangelo, the marmalade cat, had made his nest.

'Sorry Mike,' said Charlotte as she extracted her jeans from the bottom of the pile with a practised tweak. 'Time to get up.' Michaelangelo bowed gracefully to the inevitable and stalked imperiously away to see if the linen cupboard was open yet.

To say that Jessica's house was untidy would be an understatement. It was an unholy mess, a glorious chaos of plants, books and discarded clothes, interspersed with the occasional dirty coffee mug which had managed to escape the dishwasher. It's not that Jessica liked to be untidy; it just somehow happened that her possessions got the better of her and overflowed exuberantly from the various battered pine trunks and cupboards in which they were supposed to be confined.

Sometimes, when her belongings were clearly gaining on her, Jessica would have a purge, filling boxes and plastic bags to take to the Oxfam shop; but alas, the boxes rarely made it past her bedroom door and sooner or later they would be reopened when she was searching frantically for something to wear and thus insidiously re-enter circulation.

Jessica, as she readily admitted, was descended from a long line of artistic sluts: wildly creative women who painted and carved, sewed and wrote but were almost completely tone deaf. Sometimes she wondered if it was her lack of musical appreciation which had caused Oliver to reject her, but deep in her heart she feared that he couldn't cope with the chaos which was her natural habitat.

The trouble was that Jessica and Oliver had had different priorities: he had yearned for an orderly life, regular meals and a tidy house so that he could devote himself to his academic work, whereas she had always believed that beautiful colours and things were more important than order itself and that good meals and good humour were the cement which bonded people and families together. Oliver, although he enjoyed her creativity and her cooking had not been able to cope with her mess and had walked out on her before he knew that she was pregnant.

When she told him (for they remained good friends) Oliver was extremely put out.

'I thought you were on the pill, Jessica,' he had said coldly. He'd always called her Jessica but now he spoke in a voice which she had never heard before and knew she never wanted to hear again.

'I was,' she had retorted, 'but I stopped. I was worried about the risks, and besides, I wanted to have a baby. After all, I'm nearly 30'. I didn't want to leave it too late.'

'But Jessica, you knew I didn't want a child. How could you be so selfish?'

'Selfish!" she had screamed. 'Selfish! What the hell do you think *you* are Oliver?'

Oliver had sighed. He hated scenes, liking to resolve conflict by cool reasoned argument.

'Jessica,' he had begun. 'There is absolutely no question of us having a child. You must have an abortion.'

She had looked at him in amazement. This was the man she loved, the man she had thought she would marry, the father of her child. And here he was talking about it as if it was an unfortunate interruption to one of his lectures.

'Ollie,' she had begun, remembering too late how he hated to have his name abbreviated. 'Ollie. This is a baby, *our* baby, yours and mine. Doesn't that mean anything to you?'

'Jessica, my dear, I'm sorry,' he had said. 'It's out of the question, and that's final. Now, if you'll excuse me, I have to go to a meeting.'

When Oliver returned late that evening he found that Jessica had gone, leaving a sad little note.

'I'm sorry, Oliver,' she had written, 'but I want this baby, and I'm going to have it whether you want it or not. I'll always love you. Yours, Jess.'

Oliver had sighed and, after pouring himself a large whisky, had gone to bed.

It was months before they met again, before Jessica sent him a letter and the photograph of a new-born baby with the caption; Charlotte, at 10 days old. In the letter was a request that they meet to discuss the financial support of his child. Once again Oliver had sighed, but he was an honourable man and he agreed to meet her with her solicitor to discuss Charlotte's maintenance. His friends told him he was lucky that Jessica was not demanding money for herself but he knew that she was too proud to let him support her. Anyway, thought Oliver, Jessica earns more with her book illustrations and her art classes than I do at the university. She doesn't need me, he had reasoned. She'll be all right.

What Oliver never understood however, was that Jessica *did* need him because she was in love with him. She missed his quiet presence and his solid common sense. Most of all, though, she was sad that Charlotte had only one parent, that she had to admit to her friends and their parents that she had no father, that her mother was not even married.

Now that 12 years had passed, Jessica had accepted her single status. She worried less about Charlotte, too, because Oliver took her out regularly and the child had long since learned to deal with any snide remarks about her lack of a 'normal' family. 'I've got two families,' she would declare proudly and no one dared to challenge her that one was better.

Jessica and Charlotte went together to the hospital to collect Jeannie and brought her home in their ancient Citroen. Jess was appalled at the change in the old lady who seemed infinitely frailer than she had been. The younger woman had known that Joe was the strong one in their partnership but she hadn't realised quite the extent to which Jeannie had been dependent upon her husband. It was almost as though Jeannie had become a child again, so bewildered was she by Joe's illness. She confided in Jess that she and Joe had always assumed that she, Jeannie would 'go' first and that the prospect of facing life without her husband was more than she could bear.

As the days turned into weeks, however, Joe slowly began to mend. Jess took Jeannie in to see him each day and would sit, reading her book, slouched in the modern easy chairs outside the ward. It was here that, one memorable Thursday, that she chanced to meet Tom Hitchcock.

'Hello,' said Tom as he sat down gingerly opposite her. 'Didn't I see you in the Intensive Care Unit?' Jess looked up from her book and smiled. 'I'm not sure,' she said. 'Did you?'

126

'I'm sure I did,' said Tom. Then as the jigsaw fell into place he said, 'You were with Mrs Peterson when she came to visit poor old Joe. Are you their daughter?'

Jess grinned. 'No,' she said, 'I'm a neighbour.'

'And you bring her in every day?' Tom asked in a surprised voice.

'Well,' said Jess, 'there's no one else really, and she's been terribly shaken by Joe's illness.'

'What a kind girl you are,' said Tom. 'I wish I had someone like you to look after me!'

'What's wrong with you?' said Jess, then, realising that she had yet again been a little too direct, said, 'Sorry. I shouldn't have asked.'

Tom laughed. 'It's all right,' said Tom. 'I'm long past all modesty. I've had cancer of the rectum, the back passage, and they've cut it out.'

'The whole thing?' said Jess.

'Yes,' said Tom. 'I've got a colostomy. Wonderfully convenient,' he said. 'Just the thing for boating. I'll never need to go to the loo again.'

Not in the least deceived by his bravado, Jess's reply was quiet. 'That's hard,' she said. 'That's very hard.'

Tom met her gaze and she saw the pain in his eyes. 'Yes,' he said. 'It has been hard and I've had quite a struggle coming to terms with it. The nurses have been wonderful, especially Lucy, the Sister on ITU.'

Jess nodded. 'Yes,' she said. 'I thought she was pretty special.'

'She is,' said Tom. 'I was in quite a state after the operation, in one way and another and she helped me pull through, gave me a reason for living.'

Jess was surprised at this last remark. 'A reason for living?' she said.

'Yes,' said Tom. 'You see, I'm on my own these days, and for a long time I thought I'd be better off dead. I think I might well have killed myself if I'd had a chance, but there's not a lot of privacy for committing suicide under those bloody arc lights.'

Jess looked at Tom's face and her artist's eye admired the fine bone structure under his pale skin. 'What happened to your family?' she asked tentatively.

Tom laughed. A short, bitter laugh. 'Oh don't worry. You needn't be delicate. It doesn't suit you. My wife left me a year ago – she found someone she liked better. The kids are at boarding school and they spend most of the holidays with their mother so I'm all on my own now with Cuthbert here,' (he patted his belly over the colostomy bag).

'What about your friends?' said Jess. 'Don't they come to visit you?'

'I haven't really got any friends down here. You see, I left London after my marriage broke up. I tried to make a new start in Canada, but it didn't work out, so I decided to move down to the South West. I'd only been down here six weeks when they discovered that I had cancer. That was three months ago.'

'Three months,' said Jess. 'That's a long time.'

'I was very ill after the operation,' said Tom quietly. 'I had a massive pulmonary embolus, a clot on the lung. They say I nearly died. Then I became very depressed. I couldn't face the thought of the future with old Cuthbert here and without,' here his voice faltered, 'without being able to make love.'

Jess looked appalled. 'Did they, did they take that away as well?'

Tom looked at her blankly for a moment and then laughed. Not knowing quite what to do, Jess laughed too and it was a couple of minutes before they were able to pull themselves together again.

Wiping the tears from his eyes, Tom said, 'Oh bless you, Jess. I haven't laughed like that since my wife left me.' Then serious once more, he said, 'No, they didn't cut it off, thank God, but they had to cut a lot of nerves to get out all the cancer and the surgeon says it's very likely that I'll be impotent. So much for my plans for beginning life again. Who'd want to make love with an impotent man with a colostomy? It's like one of those sick jokes you find in a cheap Christmas cracker.'

Jess looked down at her lap for a moment, deeply moved and not knowing at all what was the right thing to say. Then, quietly, and tentatively, she said, 'There's more to life than sex, don't you think? I've been on my own for ten years now. It's not easy, but I get by. I think that friendship is actually much more important than sex, and being impotent wont stop you making friends.'

It was Tom's turn to look down and Jess was appalled to see a tear run down his cheek and splash on to his hands. Impulsively, she took the wet hand in hers. 'I'm sorry,' she said. 'I had no right to say all that. How can I possibly understand how you feel. I'm a crass, insensitive fool.'

'No you're not,' he said quickly. 'You're just honest.' Tom took Jess's other hand and they sat quietly together for a few moments. Then, withdrawing his hand to find a handkerchief, Tom blew his nose hard. 'Thank you so much,' he said. 'You've helped me more than you'll ever know.' He paused, and when he spoke again he seemed strangely shy. 'I'd really like to meet you again, when I'm back home, I mean. Do you think, perhaps, that we could be friends?'

Jess's heart gave an absurd little leap and she smiled gently. 'I'd like that very much,' she said. 'Very much indeed.'

As she spoke, Jeannie Peterson appeared at the door of the ward. Her face was wreathed in smiles and her step was more confident. 'They say he can come home next week, Jess,' she said excitedly. 'My Joe's coming home!'

Jess stood up and gave the old lady a hug. 'Oh Jeannie,' she said. 'I'm so pleased. That's wonderful news. I'm really happy for you.' Tom rose and made as if to leave the two women. 'Goodbye,' he said, 'and thank you.'

Jess smiled. 'I'll see you tomorrow,' she said.

He grinned, and said, 'In that case it's not goodbye, but *au revoir.*'

18

On the night following the picnic, David Meredith was woken from sleep by the sound of Susie calling him urgently. 'David! David, wake up. You're wanted on the phone. It's the hospital.'

David groaned and fought against the urge to ignore her. Suddenly he was fully awake and his throat constricted at the realisation of what this call must mean. 'Oh God,' he said. 'It'll be about Robbie.'

The landing light was on and Susie stood there dishevelled in Ben's navy and green striped towelling dressing gown. 'You'd better take it in the study, David,' she said. 'I'll come down and turn the lights on for you.'

'Father Meredith?' asked the voice, not used to calling priests by their Christian names. 'This is Staff Nurse on William Harvey Ward at the Royal Victoria Hospital. I'm sorry to disturb you, but Robbie is very poorly and he's asking for you.'

'What's happened?' asked David. 'He was fine when I brought him back this evening.'

'I know,' said Nell, 'but he's started to haemorrhage and is deteriorating rapidly.'

'I'll be with you in about 15 minutes,' said David.

'Thank you, Father,' said the nurse.

Robbie had tried hard to think clearly but he'd felt sleepy and a bit faint. He'd been bleeding – he'd felt the blood warm and damp around his buttocks when he'd woken. 'Damn,' he thought, and struggled to subdue the feelings of terror which seized him. He'd rung the bell and the nurse had come rapidly as she always did.

'Nell, I think I'm bleeding again.'

Nell had looked at his pale face and felt his pulse. It was very weak. This must be a big one. Keeping her composure she'd lifted up the bedclothes, taking care that Robbie should not see what was there. Sure enough there was a pool of blood, a scarlet lake running down between Robbie's legs and soaking into the bedclothes. Pressing the call button, she'd held Robbie's hand and waited for her junior, a quiet sensible girl called Rosalind.

'Ros,' she now said in as calm a voice as she could manage as the girl appeared at the door. 'Would you sit with Robbie for a few minutes please, while I make a phone call? Ring the bell if you need me.'

Ros looked at Robbie and smiled. 'Hello,' she said. 'What have you been up to?'

Robbie smiled warmly, but had no heart to joke. 'I'm bleeding again,' he said.

'Oh, Robbie!' Drawing up a chair, Ros sat down and took his hand in hers.

Robbie returned Ros's squeeze and lay there gripping her hand tightly.

'Oh Ros,' he said. 'I'm so frightened.'

Ros stroked the pale hand in hers and hoped that Nell would return soon. Sure enough Nell was back in a few minutes, accompanied by a tall blonde doctor in his early thirties.

Owen Davies, the haematology Registrar, knew Robbie well. 'Hello, Rob,' he said, 'how are you feeling?'

'Lousy,' said Robbie. 'Cold. Sick and a bit giddy.'

Owen felt for Robbie's pulse, it was barely palpable and very fast. The boy's face was very pale and beads of perspiration stood out on his brow. Owen turned to Nell and said more casually than he felt. 'I think we'll put up a drip and cross match a bit of blood. 'Okay, Robbie?' he turned to face the young man.

Robbie nodded, then, addressing Nell, he said, 'Could you ring my friend, Father Meredith, please. His phone number's in my address book in my locker.'

Nell bent over the locker and retrieved a small black-coated diary. 'What about your parents, Robbie?' she said. 'Do you want me to call them, too?'

Robbie's face contorted with anxiety. 'No,' he said. 'Please, please, no. I don't want them here. I couldn't cope with their fussing over me. This is hard enough anyway. I can't support them any longer. *Please* don't call them.'

'Okay, Robbie. Okay.' Owen's voice was firm. 'I promise you, we won't call them. Please don't distress yourself.'

Nell opened her mouth to say something, but closed it again when she saw Owen's face.

Robbie was less tense now and Owen was working on his hand for a vein. Eventually, he found one and, once the drip was running, Robbie relaxed visibly, and closing his eyes, drifted into sleep.

When he woke, ten minutes later, David was standing at the foot of the bed with Nell and Owen.

'Hello,' he said. 'Thank you for coming.'

David lowered himself into the chair beside the bed and took Robbie's hand. Nell glanced at Owen and the two of them withdrew into the corridor, closing the door quietly behind them.

Robbie looked up at David and tried to smile. Instead, he said faintly, 'It's bad, this time, David, isn't it?'

David fought to keep back his tears. 'Yes, Robbie, I think it is. But the blood's on its way and they're going to give you some more platelets.'

Robbie was quiet for a moment, then he said in a voice that was barely audible. 'I don't think it's going to work this time. I think this is it.'

David's tears fell wetly on to his hand and Robbie's but he paid no heed to them. The boy's hand looked almost transparent and his voice was very faint. He was saying something now, and David bent over him to hear.

'Tell . . . tell Katie that I love her,' he said. 'Tell her that she must live for both of us.'

David gulped. 'I'll tell her, Robbie,' he said. 'Do you want me to get her now?'

Robbie shook his head. 'No,' he said. 'Just you.' He closed his eyes and appeared to sleep, his hand limp in David's.

David sat quietly at the bedside, his heart full of anguish yet somehow peaceful in the soft light of the small room. The nurses had put up the first unit of blood and changed the blood stained sheets but the smell of stale blood remained. Nell had warned David that Robbie was likely to haemorrhage again at any time and had left a dark red towel on a chair at the foot of the bed. After about an hour had passed Robbie opened his eyes again and seeing David dozing in the chair beside him squeezed the older man's hand weakly. David opened his eyes and smiled.

'Hello, Rob,' he said. 'How are you feeling?'

'Peaceful,' said Robbie quietly. 'Very peaceful. Very happy.'

Strangely shaken by this last remark, David sat quietly for a moment, then he said softly, 'Are you afraid, Robbie?'

The boy smiled, his face pale and gaunt against the pillows. 'Not now,' he said. 'Not any more.'

David held the thin hand in his and marvelled at the grace of the past few days. What a long way they had travelled together, what an amazing journey.

For another hour Robbie slept peacefully, his hand loose in David's, while the older man slept and prayed in the easy chair beside the bed. From time to time Nell came quietly in to check that the drip was running and that Robbie was at peace. By a strange coincidence it was while Nell was there that things changed.

After sleeping peacefully for an hour, Robbie gradually became restless and somehow troubled. David looked inquiringly at Nell but she made no move. Suddenly it happened. Robbie gave a little cry and, struggling to sit up, reached for the vomit bowl on the locker beside him. Nell moved rapidly. 'Push the bell please, Father,' she said, and taking the towel put her arm behind Robbie's back to help him sit up. 'Get in behind him,' she said quietly to David. 'Support him against your chest.'

Slipping his left arm behind Robbie's shoulders, David took the frail body in his arms, supporting him against his chest while Nell held the vomit bowl and the red towel to mop up the scarlet tide from Robbie's mouth.

Ros, who had witnessed a similar death two weeks before sat quietly on the foot of the bed with a fresh supply of cardboard bowls in one hand and a tray containing sedative drugs in the other.

After a couple of minutes she put the tray down. There would be no need for drugs now. Robbie's battle, fought with such courage and youthful determination, was drawing rapidly towards its close.

Robbie lay limply in David's arms now, supported on the priest's chest. David thanked God that it had all been so fast, that the boy had lost consciousness almost at once. He looked at Nell and saw that the tears were running silently down her cheeks. Their eyes met and Nell said quietly, 'He's gone now. We'll lie him down.'

Together they took Robbie's lifeless body in their arms and lay him gently down. Taking a flannel Nell wiped the blood from his face and laid a clean towel over the stained sheets. Then, haltingly, she said to David, 'Would you say a prayer for him, Father?'

David sat quietly by the bed and with his hand on Robbie's said the only prayer that seemed fitting for such a moment; a prayer of thankfulness for the gift of Robbie's life and courage, his generosity and his humour. He prayed, too, for Katie, whose friendship and love had brought a new meaning to Robbie's last days, and for his parents who had loved him so much that he had not wanted them to witness his passing. Lastly, David prayed for himself, for Nell and Ros, and for all whose lives are somehow caught up in the terrifying mysteries of life and death.

Katie woke to a light August morning with the sun shining brightly. She lay still in her hospital bed and looked up at the ceiling. How plain it all was, she thought, but somehow familiar and safe. Reliving in her mind the events of the previous day she marvelled at the gift that had been given her. Never before had she met a man like Robbie. He had a tenderness, a vulnerability and an openness which was quite new to her. She was used to men who were smart and aggressive, who drank rather too much beer and drove their cars too fast. Men such as these would have considered Robbie a bit odd, something of a wimp. At one time she might have agreed with them, but now she knew differently. Robbie was the bravest man she had never met, the bravest she was ever likely to meet.

She smiled to herself and wondered what they would do today. David had promised to be in around ten so that they could meet and plan their day. She looked at her watch – seven o'clock. Only three hours to go. She closed her eyes and allowed herself to drift back into that delicious stage of being half awake yet half asleep when the mind has free range and dreams can sometimes be continued at will.

As Katie dozed she felt the sun warm on her face and the warmth of Robbie's jacket beneath her head. She remembered the gentleness with which he had touched her and the look of awe and reverence upon his face when she had allowed him to explore her body. She had wished that she could have given him more, but that had not been possible. Perhaps one day, who knows. She stopped herself abruptly. 'Take it one day at a time Katie,' he'd said. 'None of us can count on tomorrow. Let's just be grateful for today.'

She slept again and woke to find David Meredith sitting by her bed.

'Hello!' she began, 'Isn't it a wonderful day? What shall . . .' she stopped in mid-sentence, seeing for the first time that David was unshaven and had massive shadows under his eyes. She sat bolt upright. 'What's wrong, David?' she said. 'What's happened? Tell me. I want to know.'

David smiled. Poor Katie. How was he to find words to tell her that Robbie was dead? 'Katie,' he began, 'I'm afraid . . .'

She interrupted him with a soft moan. 'Oh, God. He's dead, isn't he? I can tell from your face. He's dead. Oh David. I can't bear it . . .'

David took her in his arms and held her as she wept, his own tears falling unheeded into her hair. Feeling her thin shoulders beneath her night dress, he was reminded of Robbie and he prayed angrily to the God who deals out death as well as life.

'Couldn't you have given them more time?' he asked. 'Just a few weeks. What are a few weeks to you? Why did you have to take him away from her so soon?'

There was a quiet knock on the door and Debbie came in with a tray of tea. She laid it down on the bedside and looked searchingly at Katie. 'Hello, Katie,' she said. 'I'm so sorry. Is there anything I can do for you?' Katie shook her head and Debbie withdrew, telling them to ring if there was anything they wanted.

David and Katie sat in silence as they drank their tea, united by grief and their shared experience. When Katie had finished she put the cup down and, looking at the priest said, 'David. Do you think I could see him? To say goodbye.'

David looked at Katie's tear-stained face. How different she looked from yesterday when she had been dressed, with her hair done and her lipstick in place. Today she looked strangely like

Robbie, pale and thin with the hollow-eyed look which illness brings.

'Of course, Katie,' he said. 'I rather thought you might, so I asked the nurses if you could. Would you like to go now, before his parents arrive?'

Katie nodded. 'Would you hand me my dressing gown, please.' David handed her the gown on the back of the door and after Katie had combed her hair they made their way slowly towards the lift.

Di Ashton, the ward sister, met them at the door of William Harvey Ward. 'Hello Katie,' she said. 'I'm so sorry.'

Katie smiled briefly and together the three of them made their way to the side ward where Robbie's body lay.

The room was more orderly now than David remembered it. Clearly, the nurses had been tidying up. Robbie's body lay neatly in the middle of the bed, his face transparently pale. The room smelled of air freshener mixed with the sickly smell of vomited blood. Appalled, Katie felt sick, and put her hand up to her mouth. Seeing her expression, David put his arm lightly around her shoulders. Together they approached the bed. Katie put out her hand to touch the pale face. Her hand ran lightly down the cheek until she felt the faint stubble of his beard. Suddenly, as if this reminder of his kiss was too much, she wheeled around to face the priest, the tears streaming down her face. 'He's not there, David. He's gone. He's not there.'

David held her firmly to his chest and stroked her hair until the sobs trailed away, then, supporting her elbow led her out of the room without a backward glance.

Sitting huddled in Di's office Katie clutched yet another mug of tea. David sat quietly while she talked, first about how she felt about Robbie and then about her earlier life. She told him about her first relationship, of how she had fallen head over heels in love at 15 and been an unmarried mother at 16. At first it had seemed that she and Steve would be happy, but then he lost his job and his drinking, already heavy, became a major problem. It was when he was drunk that the violence had begun. At first it was verbal, but then, one night when he was very drunk, he had hit her, giving her a black eye. She had been shattered and had threatened to leave him, but he had begged her to give him another chance and she had relented.

For the next few months all had been quiet. He had looked hard for a job, but had had no luck. Then one cold Saturday afternoon he had lost his temper. Irritated by the seemingly endless array of nappies drying in front of the gas fire, he had begun to shout at her and two-year-old Emma. Katie remembered the scene all too well. The toddler screaming and clinging to her skirt while Steve hurled abuse at her. Eventually, he could bear her cries no longer and had taken hold of Emma by her arm and shaken her until the screams turned to terrified moans. Katie had rushed at her to rescue the child and he had hit her hard across the face, splitting her lip. Desperate, Katie had gone at him like a tigress, scratching his face and beating her hands on his chest, screaming at the same time for help.

What would have happened if the neighbours had not come to her rescue, Katie never knew. The police had been called and Steve taken away to sober up. Katie and Emma had been placed in a refuge for battered wives until things could be sorted out.

Once more Steve had begged Katie to take him back but she had refused. The social worker told her that Emma had been put on the 'At Risk' Register and that if Katie returned to Steve and there was considered risk of further violence, the child would be taken into care. Katie had seen the wisdom of their judgement and had, with a sad heart, told Steve that they must separate.

David's heart was heavy as he listened to her tale. It was not that he had not heard such sadness before – indeed it was all too familiar – but it seemed now doubly cruel that her time with Robbie had been so brief. Eventually, Katie wearied of talking and David asked her gently what she would like to do now.

She looked up at him, her face blotchy and swollen with tears and whispered, 'I can't face going back to the ward at the moment. I'm sorry. I just can't cope.'

David nodded. He understood. He too would have found it hard to return to a public ward. He hesitated, then, trusting what he knew of Susie's generous hospitality, asked Katie whether she would like to spend the day at Susie's.

Katie's excitement was pathetic. 'Oh,' she said. 'Do you think I could? It's such a wonderful house, and she *so* kind.'

'I'll ring her and ask,' said David. 'Will you be okay here on your own for a while while I go and find a phone?' Katie nodded and David left her, looking more than ever waif like, in the bare hospital office.

Susie came out to the car to meet them, and putting her arm around Katie, led her into the house. Once inside, Katie threw herself into Susie's ample arms and clung there weeping like a child. Susie held her tightly until the harshest of her weeping subsided and then led her gently up the stairs into a brightly furnished bedroom. Pulling back the bed covers to reveal a hot water bottle in a funny cover, Susie helped the exhausted girl into bed. Taking a large, old fashioned teddy bear off a battered dressing table she tucked him under the covers beside Katie.

'Big Ted will look after you,' she said firmly. 'He understands all about broken hearts.'

There was a brief pause and then a thin arm took hold of Ted's outstretched paw and he disappeared under the bed clothes.

'Now, Katie.' Susie knelt by the bed. 'How would it be if I come and wake you up in time to have a bath before lunch?'

Katie smiled. 'That would be lovely,' she said. 'Thank you so much.'

Susie smiled and bending over, kissed Katie lightly on the forehead. 'Sleep well,' she said. 'David and I will be downstairs if you need us.' Drawing the curtains to shut out the brightest of the sunlight, she went out and closed the door gently.

When Susie returned to her kitchen she found David sitting wearily at the kitchen table with his head in his hands. This time it was David's turn to feel the warmth of Susie's arm around his shoulders.

'Hello,' he said wearily, 'I was having a little nap.'

'Perhaps I should put you straight to bed as well,' she said, but he shook his head.

'I need some coffee,' he said, 'and maybe some scrambled eggs.'

David drank his coffee and ate his breakfast in an apparently abstracted silence. Susie bided her time. He would talk about it when he was ready. At last, when his eggs were finished and his coffee mug recharged. David lit a cigarette and inhaled deeply.

'Oh, Susie,' he said. 'What a night.'

'Do you want to talk about it,' said Susie quietly, 'or is it too terrible to recall?'

'No,' said David. 'It wasn't really terrible, just unbelievably sad. He bled to death, Susie just exsanguinated in my arms. The blood was all over the bed and I was left holding this white shell that used to be Robbie. He looked like Jesus in Michaelangelo's *Pieta*, and I felt like his mum. God it hurt.'

Susie laid her hand over his for a moment but said nothing. 'That was my side of it,' said David. 'I think that for Robbie it was all right, except for those last terrible moments.' He paused, stubbed out his cigarette and began again. 'It was amazing, really,' he said. 'He knew he was going to die, and yet he was completely at peace, quite unafraid. It's as though he received some special grace, a strength and dignity to cope with those last few hours.'

'Did Katie see him die?' asked Susie.

'No, thank God. Robbie didn't want her there. Perhaps he had some intuition that things were going to get messy. He knew a lot about leukaemia.' said David. 'He knew he was at risk of bleeding to death. That had always been on the cards, and he was always afraid of it.'

'What about his parents?'

'He was adamant that he didn't want them either. He felt he couldn't cope with them fussing over him. So we didn't call them.'

Susie whistled softly. 'How did they feel about that?'

'No one told them that he didn't want them there. The doctors and nurses explained that it all happened very quickly. They were too stunned to worry about the timing of it all.'

'Did you have a chance to talk to them?' asked Susie.

'Briefly. I'll go and see them at home tomorrow when they've had a chance to get over the initial shock of it all.'

'Poor things. To lose an only son, and such a lovely lad.'

'I know,' said David, 'though the truth is, I think they lost him a while back, by trying to hold on to him too tightly. Robbie couldn't cope with the way his mother tried to mollycoddle him.'

Susie sighed. 'How difficult it is,' she said. 'If you try to give your kids space you wonder if they'll think you don't love them . . .'

'And if you love them too much they reject you! I know,' said David. 'You can't win.'

'What do you intend to do about Katie?' asked Susie. 'Do you want me to let her stay here for a few days?'

David paused. 'No,' he said. 'I think she should go back to the hospital when she's composed herself. What I had wondered, though, is whether you'd be prepared to see her professionally for a while. I know she's seen a psychiatrist briefly but I doubt he'd have time to see her on a regular basis. I've got a hunch that she'd really benefit from some therapy.'

Susie was quiet and David began to roll another cigarette. He looked across at Susie who was fiddling quietly with her napkin. 'Is that asking too much?' he said. 'I know how busy you are.'

'No,' said Susie quietly. 'That's fine. I think that would be really good. Have you mentioned it to her?'

'No, of course not,' said David. 'I wouldn't do that without asking.'

'No, I know you wouldn't. Sorry, I wasn't thinking. I'll wait for you to choose your moment then.'

'Susie, you're an angel'

Susie grinned. 'I do my best, Father,' she said. 'Now, why don't you go and have a bath and a shave and a little nap, and I'll see you at lunch time. Leave Katie to me. I'll look after her.'

19

It was four-thirty on Christmas Eve when Macmillan Nurse, Victoria Woodhouse, drew up outside number 25 Alexander Road. She had left Joe and Jeannie until last so that she could spend a little extra time with the old lady who, as Joe's condition worsened, was becoming increasingly dependent upon her.

She rang the bell and the door was opened by Jeannie's neighbour, Tom Hitchcock, who had recently moved in with Jessica.

'Hello, Tom,' said Victoria. 'Happy Christmas. How are you?'

Tom grinned. 'I'm fine,' he said, 'just fine, but poor old Joe's not so good. Jeannie rang us first thing this morning and Jess has been in and out all day.'

'Jess is an angel!' said Victoria. 'Are you sure it's not too much for her?'

'No,' said Tom, 'She seems to be thriving on it. She sees it as a way of saying "thank you" for the happiness of the past few months. If Jeannie hadn't asked her to help when she was visiting Joe, then we'd never have met, and, well . . . you know the rest.'

Victoria smiled. 'I know,' she said. 'I'm so happy for the two of you.'

Victoria took off her coat and laid it over a chair in the hallway. 'I'll go up then,' she said, 'and see how things are.'

Victoria tapped gently on the bedroom door and as she entered, Jeannie rose slowly from her chair beside the bed. 'Oh nurse,' she said. 'I'm so glad you've come. Joe's been so poorly.'

Jess, who had been standing behind the old lady put her arm around her shoulders. 'Why don't you come and let Tom make you a cup of tea, Jeannie?' she said quietly, 'while nurse sees to Joe. I'll tell her what's been happening.'

Jess led the exhausted old lady into the spare bedroom and sat her down in the armchair by the window. 'Will you be all right, Jeannie?' she said. 'Tom'll be up in a minute with some tea.'

Jeannie nodded and, raising a withered hand, pushed back a strand of grey hair from her forehead. 'Thank you, my dear,' she said. 'You two are so good to us. I don't know what I'd do without you. You're like a daughter to me.' Jess bent over and kissed the old lady gently on the forehead. 'It's no trouble,' she said. 'Now sit there and rest for a minute.'

After calling down to ask Tom to make a pot of tea, Jess returned to the other bedroom to see if Victoria needed any help. She found the nurse kneeling at the side of the double bed, her ear close to the old man's face. Jess sat quietly on the end of the bed.

'No, Joe. It won't be long now,' Victoria was saying. 'Are you afraid?'

The old man shook his head. 'I worry about Jeannie, though,' he said, so faintly that Victoria could barely catch his words.

Jess joined the nurse kneeling beside the bed. She took the old man's hand. 'Joe, darling,' she said softly but firmly. 'You're *not* to worry about Jeannie. I've told you that Tom and I will make sure she's all right.' Joe looked at Jess, his dark hollow eyes misting with tears, then he smiled and closed his eyes and seemed to sleep.

Jess and Victoria moved across to the window alcove and sat on the seat below it. 'He's very weak now,' said Jess.

'I know,' said Victoria. 'Would you like me to see if there's a bed in the hospice?'

Jessica shook her head firmly. 'No,' she said. 'It would break their hearts to be separated. They've been together for the last 60 years and we mustn't part them now. God knows, it'll happen soon enough.'

Victoria smiled. 'They're very lucky to have you, Jess,' she said. 'After all, you're no relation, are you?'

Jess grinned. 'No,' she said. 'My parents were very different. But I've known Joe and Jeannie for the past ten years or so and I'm very fond of them. I'm happy to be able to do something for them.'

Victoria smiled again. 'Right,' she said. 'I'd better go and have a word with Jeannie.'

'Shall I come?' said Jess. 'Or would you rather be on your own with her?'

'No, I think it would be good if you were there. She probably won't take in much of what I say.'

'Poor lamb,' said Jess. 'She's dead on her feet. She hasn't had a proper night's sleep since Joe came home from hospital.'

The two women entered the spare bedroom and sat down beside the old lady who was staring blankly at her cup of tea. 'Oh, Jeannie,' said Victoria, taking the old lady's hand. 'You look so tired. What are we going to do with you?'

Jeannie's eyes filled with tears. 'It won't be much longer now, will it nurse?' she said. 'There'll be time enough to sleep when he's gone.'

Victoria was silent for a moment. 'No, my love,' she said quietly, 'I'm afraid it won't be long.'

The tears ran unchecked down Jeannie's face. 'He's all I have in the world,' she said. 'There's no one else. No one.'

Victoria sat quietly, holding the old lady's hand. After a while, she spoke. 'Jeannie,' she said. 'I know how you feel, but you *must* get some rest. If I get a nurse to come for the nights, will you promise me that you'll go to bed and try to sleep?'

Jeannie sat with her head bowed. 'He like's me there,' she muttered.

Victoria sighed. 'I know, sweetheart,' she said, 'but if you don't get some sleep you'll crack up, and then where will you be?'

There was a pause, then Jeannie spoke. 'What sort of a nurse?' she said. 'A *proper* nurse'

Victoria smiled. 'Yes,' she said. 'A *proper* nurse and it won't cost you anything. The Marie Curie nurses are nurses who sit with cancer patients and their families when they're very poorly. She'll stay with Joe all night so that you and Jess here can get some rest.'

'What,' said Jeannie slowly, 'what if something happens in the night? Will she call me?'

Victoria took a deep breath. 'Jeannie, love,' she said, '*of course* she'll call you. You'll be sleeping in here, just a few feet away from him.'

Jeannie said nothing for a few moments, but then she sighed and said, 'All right. I suppose you're right. I can't go on like this. When will she come?'

'I'll go and telephone the office,' said Victoria, and see if I can get someone for tonight, and rising from her knees, she went out of the room, leaving the old lady with Jess.

Having arranged for a Marie Curie nurse to come in each night at nine o'clock for the next few days, Victoria bid Joe and Jeannie

143

good night. She spent half an hour drinking tea and eating Christmas cake with Tom and Jess and then, promising to visit immediately after Christmas, she took her leave.

Victoria loved Christmas and looked forward to spending the holiday with her partner Bill and their various children. One of a small team of specialist nurses working in the community, she provided a consultative service to general practitioners and their district nurses but was not directly on call for her patients outside normal working hours. Although there was always a doctor on call 24 hours a day for any patient, the reality was that this cover rarely met the needs of anxious families who needed a continuity of care which simply was not possible. When Victoria had begun working as a Macmillan nurse ten years before, she had always given patients her home telephone number and permission to call her if they were worried. At first, the out of hours calls had not worried her, but as the months turned into years she had found herself becoming chronically tired and irritable and generally less like her usual cheerful energetic source.

When her husband left her for another woman five years previously she had become clinically depressed and during discussions with her doctor Victoria had come to realise that her pattern of work, although apparently wonderfully dedicated, was in reality quite unrealistic. 'Working at that pace is fine for emergencies,' she had said. 'If there's a major disaster we all expect to work around the clock, but you're a marathon runner, not a sprinter. If you don't pace yourself you'll never stay the course.'

At first, Victoria had been angry. 'You don't understand,' she had said. 'My patients are *dying*. They're frightened and desperate. They *need* me. They can't keep their pain and their distress to office hours. Their being able to phone me out of hours is essential to the service I provide.'

Her doctor had sighed. 'Victoria,' she had said gently, 'If you go on working at this pace, denying your own humanity and your need for time off you'll burn out. Why do you think Roy left you? Could it be that you gave so much of yourself to your patients that there wasn't enough left over for him?'

Victoria had wept long and hard but when the time came for her to go back to work she arranged her life differently. With her GP's help she had come to realise that, however much she cared about her patients, she needed her time off if she was to survive. Little by little she came to see herself as a member of the health care team and not as the only person who really cared about her patients. It had been a hard lesson to learn, and quite humbling, but she was much calmer and happier now and found that she was coping with her work with a lot less strain.

As she drove home, Victoria replayed the day's events. Unlike the district nurses who saw many different patients each day, giving injections, dressing wounds and other 'hands on' nursing procedures, Victoria saw relatively few patients and most of them were terminally ill with cancer. Her work involved not so much basic nursing as the highly specialised issues of pain and symptom control and general supportive care of the patient and family.

Important as the symptom control side of her work was, Victoria found that the emotional support she gave the whole family was what made her work so special. Time and again she had seen families devastated by a terminal illness gradually come to terms with their grief and face their impending loss with courage and dignity. She was constantly moved by the reserves of strength and generosity in the hearts of ordinary men and women who, when properly supported, were able to care for a dying family member with a dedication and competence that they did not know they possessed.

Particularly rewarding were the situations in which the conspiracy of silence had caused a rift between his or her carers. The myth that a patient would 'give up' and die if he knew that his illness was incurable was still widespread, though the reality, as Victoria knew well, is that a policy of deliberate lying in which families tried to conceal from a patient that he or she was dying leads only to tension and loneliness. The families would try to keep a brave face so that the dying person would not suspect the seriousness of his situation and in so doing would deny him the opportunity to voice his fears or ventilate the anger and grief which welled up in his heart.

Such situations of collusion were difficult to manage, requiring infinite patience and finesse. Once resolved, however, and the patient and his loved ones were able to communicate openly, the tension usually vanished. Paradoxically, although a patient might be physically deteriorating, the quality of his life often improved dramatically because he did not have to bottle up his emotions and because he knew himself loved.

Victoria decided to go home via the city centre in the hope that the fairy lights and last minute shoppers would banish all thoughts of work and death and kindle a little Christmas cheer in her heart. It was not that she was sad or depressed, just pensive with her heart very full of the pain of those she had visited that day.

Mary and John Carlisle were coping well now, thank God. What a terrible few months it had been for them. At first they had been full of hope, determined to 'fight' the cancer but after two months of chemotherapy, Dr Radcliffe had seen the two of them together to explain that the drugs were not working and that her disease was progressing in spite of treatment so that further chemotherapy would not be appropriate.

Victoria had taken over the support of Mary and John and their family from that point. The first few weeks had not been easy, for Mary was devastated by what was happening to her and wanted to do nothing but sit at home all day while John was determined that they should 'fight' the disease and wanted Mary to try all manner of way-out diets and treatments. John, in particular, found it hard to accept Victoria's help. He didn't want her to see Mary on her own lest she talk about death and destroy his wife's hope. Little by little however, he came to value Victoria's expertise and his hostility melted away.

Mercifully, they now had a very good relationship and though Mary was quite unwell the family was very united and peaceful. Victoria had left John and the children busily preparing for Christmas Day while Mary lay on the sofa directing operations and giving advice about the heating of mince pies and the length of time it would take for the turkey to cook.

Dr Howard had been very supportive to both of them, and he and Victoria kept in close touch. As she drove, Victoria remembered that she had been invited to call in to the surgery for wine and mince pies, and the thought raising her spirits, turned left at the traffic lights, and drew up outside the health centre.

20

Dr Michael Howard had just finished dictating his letters when Caroline popped her head around his door. 'How are you doing?' she asked. 'The mince pies are getting cold.'

Michael looked up and grinned. 'I'm on my way,' he said. 'Don't let those greedy colleagues of ours eat them all.'

'Don't worry,' said Caroline, 'there's lots. Victoria's just arrived and Chris Walker said he'd look in on his way home if he finished in time.'

'Oh, good,' said Michael. 'I've got a bottle of whisky for him. He's been so good to Jane.'

'How *is* Jane these days?' asked Caroline. 'I haven't seen her for a while.'

'She's fine now, thank God,' said Michael. The antidepressants have really worked a treat. 'She's her old self now.'

'That must be a relief,' said Caroline. 'I'm so glad. I'm going back to the party,' she said. 'Don't be long now.'

It was nearly seven o'clock when Chris Walker arrived at the surgery, to find that most of the practice staff had gone to their respective homes. Caroline, who was helping the receptionists clear up greeted him warmly. 'Hi,' she said, 'just in time,' and handed him a glass of lukewarm mulled wine.

Chris sat down wearily and took a large gulp of the wine.

'Heavy day?' said Caroline.

'Chris nodded. 'I've been out on a domiciliary visit all afternoon,' he said, 'we were trying to decide whether or not to section a poor old man who is determined to commit suicide.'

'Not one of ours, I hope,' said Caroline.

'No,' said Chris, 'he's from another practice. His wife died a couple of weeks ago and he can't see any reason for living.'

'What about the children?' asked Caroline.

'There aren't any,' said Chris wearily, 'and no friends either, as far as I can see. Half of me wonders if the kindest thing would be to let him kill himself and be done with it. He's quite clear minded, just terribly sad.'

'What did you do in the end,' asked Caroline.

'We sectioned him,' said Chris. 'At least he'll be warm and have company for Christmas.'

'What about you?' said Caroline. 'Who've you got for Christmas?'

Chris grimaced. 'Rosie's mother arrives tonight,' he said. 'Sam has been scrubbed and polished till he shines and I'll have to mind my Ps and Qs.'

Caroline grinned. 'Rather you than me,' she said. 'I'd have thought you'd have a secret spell for dealing with mothers-in-law!'

'Not this one,' said Chris. 'Why do you think I'm still loitering here on Christmas Eve!'

He stood up and drained his wine to the dregs and then, taking a teaspoon, proceeded to eat all the bits of fruit and spice left in the glass.

'Well,' he said. 'I'd better be getting home. Happy Christmas, Caroline. See you in the New Year.' Clasping his bottle of whisky lovingly to his chest, he left Caroline to her clearing up.

'Good night, Katie,' said Susie, warmly. 'Thank you so much for the wine. I hope you have a very happy Christmas.'

Katie smiled. 'We'll be fine,' she said. 'Emma's decorated the flat and she's determined to help me cook the turkey!'

'Good for her!' said Susie. 'See you after the New Year.' As she spoke, the telephone rang in the hall and Susie heard Ben answer it and say, 'Hello, David. Happy Christmas to you too.'

Susie stood for a moment in her doorway, watching Katie walk quickly down the street towards the park. What a long way that girl's come since August, she thought. Somehow that brief relationship with Robbie had transformed her life. The fact that he had left her his flat, car and a small legacy had not only changed her circumstances financially but was irrefutable proof that she had been precious to him. Robbie had known that, after his death, she might begin to doubt the reality of his love, torment herself by thinking that it was not love but pity which had moved him. Determined that she should remember how much he had loved her, he had stipulated that at least three hundred pounds of her inheritance should be spent upon a piece of jewellery which she should consider as his special gift to her.

When the money came through, Katie had asked Susie if next time David came to stay, the three of them could go shopping together to choose her present. David had come for a few days in late November and they had had a wonderful afternoon shopping. Now, Katie was wearing a beautiful antique emerald ring on the third finger of her right hand, a reminder day in, day out, that she, Katie Roberts, was loved and therefore loveable.

'Ah, here, she is. I'll hand you over.' Ben, a blue and white striped cook's apron tied around his middle, and his hands covered in flour from making mince pies, handed Susie the receiver.

Susie lowered her bulk gratefully into the hall chair. 'Hi,' she said. 'Merry Christmas.'

Jane was being quietly sick in the privacy of the bathroom when Michael walked into the bedroom in search of her.

'Hello,' he said. 'What's up?'

Wiping her face with a damp flannel, Jane smiled at her husband. 'Nothing, darling,' she said. 'I was just being a bit sick.'

Michael looked at his wife with a worried frown. She looked well enough. Thank God she'd been so much better the last couple of months. In fact they both had. When the antidepressants had begun to work Chris had suggested that he and Jane take a week's holiday together. So he had found a last minute package holiday to Majorca and, leaving Jane's mother in charge of their protesting children, had flown off from Gatwick in search of sunshine and adventure.

It had been a blissful week. They had walked in the mountains, lain on the beach, explored tiny fishing villages and come back to their hotel each night mildly tipsy on warm Balearic air and good red wine. On the second night of the holiday, their passion rekindled, they had made love with a tenderness and leisure that they had not known for years. Later, much later, when she leafed through her diary, Jane decided that it was probably that night that Lizzie had been conceived.

Jane had suspected that she was pregnant early in December but had decided to wait until she was sure before saying anything to her husband. Now, Christmas Eve, seemed a good time to tell him, so she sat him gently down on the end of the bed and told him that they were to have another baby in June. Michael, lost for words, sat in silence for a few moments. Then, putting his arms around his wife, he drew her gently to him and held her tightly, his face buried in her hair.

When, at last, the children had gone to bed, John and Mary Carlisle sat together on their sofa, gazing into the fire.

'John,' said Mary, interrupting his reverie, 'shall we turn the lights out? I love to look at the Christmas tree in the dark.'

John rose without speaking, and after turning out the lights, rejoined his wife on the sofa.

'John,' said Mary quietly, 'I love you very much. You know that, don't you?' John put his hand out in the semi-darkness and took his wife's hand. The tears ran down his cheeks as he realised, yet again, that this was the last Christmas they would have together. He put his hand up to his face to wipe away the tears and Mary, realising what was happening spoke again. 'John, sweetheart,' she said. 'Try not to grieve too much. We've been so lucky, really, we've had such good times together, and as a family.'

John blew his nose hard. 'I don't know how I'm going to manage without you,' he said, his voice broken with emotion. 'I just don't know what I'll do.'

Mary stroked his hand. 'You'll be all right,' she said. 'You'll cope. You know you will. You always do. You're the "strong" one.'

'But Mary,' he said, 'it's not just me, it's the kids. How in God's name can I work full time and bring up two children?'

There was a long pause while neither of them spoke and they held hands tightly as if the physical act of clinging to each other could prevent their being parted. At last, it was Mary who broke the silence. 'John,' she said in a firm voice. 'I think you should re-marry.'

John gasped. The thought had indeed crossed his mind, but he had pushed it guiltily away, feeling that the very thought was being unfaithful to Mary. Now that she had raised the idea, however, he found it impossible to contemplate.

'But Mary, darling,' he began.

'No, John,' she said firmly. 'I want you to listen to me. I've

150

thought this through very carefully. You're still young and you will need a wife just as much as the children will need a mother. You mustn't think of it as disloyalty to me. I know that you love me and I know that you would never be unfaithful to me while I'm alive. But when I'm gone it will be quite different.' She paused, and taking both his hands in hers, she faced him in the soft light. 'Promise me you'll think about it, John. Promise me?'

John smiled at his wife. What an amazing woman she was. 'My darling,' he said, kissing her gently. 'I promise.'

It was midnight before Katie turned out her light. She and Emma had filled stockings for the two little ones, and when Emma had gone to bed Katie had carefully filled a stocking for her eldest daughter. The sock was a dark green woollen one, part of her inheritance from Robbie. She sat cross-legged on the big brass bed in what had been his bedroom. She loved this room so much, and felt his presence here more strongly than anywhere else in the flat. It was here, on this bed, that he had struggled with facing the fact that he might not recover from his illness, here that he had lain awake, frightened and alone. 'You'll never be alone again, Robbie,' she said to him, 'and neither shall I. You are here in my heart, and I am in yours.'

Robbie's bequest to her of his flat and car and his small savings had come as a complete surprise to Katie. He had not mentioned it to her, but just before he died had asked David to find him a solicitor so that he could make a new will in her favour.

The flat was the other side of town to where Katie had lived, in a much nicer area. It occupied the upper floor of a once gracious Georgian house overlooking a large park. The children were overjoyed. They had been happy enough playing in the yard of the council flats where Katie had lived before, but this was something else. They kept pinching themselves as if to make sure that it was not all a dream.

By a curious coincidence, the house was not far from where Susie lived and on a fine day she could pick out the chimneys of Susie's house from her bedroom window.

Katie had been in therapy with Susie for four months now, and they met each Wednesday afternoon at Susie's place, in her study at the back of the big town house. At first, Katie had found the meetings strange. She was not used to talking about herself, indeed she was not used to anyone listening to her for more than a couple of minutes at a time. For the first month Katie talked only of Robbie, of her grief at his death, and of her gratitude to him. She could not believe that Robbie had left all these things to her, and felt sure that his parents would find some reason why she should not have them. Little by little, however, she accepted that this was what Robbie had wanted and determined that she should not betray his trust in her.

When the initial intensity of Katie's grief had abated, Susie began to explore Katie's world with her. It was as though Susie held the younger woman's hand as she retraced her steps along the alleyways of the past. They dealt briefly with her relationship with her most recent partner, but spent much longer on her first and second partners and the difficulties she had encountered. To Katie's surprise, Susie expressed the most interest of all in her childhood, and in her relationship with her parents, especially with her father. Katie told Susie of how her father's disciplining of her had led to sexual abuse. At first it was difficult to talk about what had happened and Katie felt deeply ashamed. Little by little, however, in the safety of Susie's comfortable little room, Katie allowed herself once again to remember the events in detail.

She told Susie of how, desperate for affection, she had fallen in love with Steve, who was several years older than herself, and become pregnant by him while she was only 16. At first it had been wonderful to escape from her father, but it was not long before the violence that forced her to leave him began.

Alone with a small child in a dreary high rise council flat Katie was bitterly lonely and, yearning for affection as she did, fell again and again into unsatisfactory relationships. By the time she was 20, Katie had another small child, and had resigned herself to the world in which she lived.

As the weeks went by and Susie became more familiar with the grey sheets and dark alleyways of Katie's former life, she marvelled at the young woman's resilience, that she remained trusting and full of hope in spite of all that had happened to her. Her relationship with Robbie seemed nothing short of miraculous, for it had given Katie what she needed most, a sense of her own worth.

That Christmas Eve, after they had exchanged Christmas greetings and personal news over the telephone, Susie told David how pleased she was with Katie's progress. 'She's doing wonderfully well,' she said. 'She's found the therapy heavy going but she's got a lot of insight and is very quick to learn. I have high hopes for her.'

'That's great,' said David thoughtfully. 'My one fear is that she'll get lonely again and get caught up in another unsatisfactory relationship. History has a nasty way of repeating itself.'

'I know,' said Susie, 'but we've looked at this issue and she's well aware of her vulnerability. My great hope is that she'll learn to cope with being on her own while she works out who she is and what she wants out of life for herself and the kids. My hunch is she'll be okay, David.'

David grinned. 'Susie,' he said, 'I'd trust my life to your hunches. You're the Miss Marple of psychotherapy.'

'Get lost,' said Susie lovingly. 'Now, I must go and attend to my wifely duties! Happy Christmas.'

David Meredith smiled as he put the phone down. He was enormously fond of Susie and he had been quite serious when he'd told her that he trusted her hunches. She was a wise woman and an extremely shrewd therapist, as he himself had found out many years before when he and Susie had been in a professional relationship.

David lit a cigarette and putting his feet on the coffee table thought back to his first meeting with Susie. They had both been in their forties then, David in the throes of what he laughingly called his 'mid-life crisis,' and Susie a much sought after psychotherapist. David, who had not wanted to have therapy, and had been convinced that he could handle his problems on his own had been requested by his religious superiors to meet Susie for at least one interview. Reluctantly, he had gone, convinced that he was wasting his time and that a female psychotherapist who was also an atheist could not possibly understand the problems of a middle-aged Jesuit who was having difficulties adjusting to life in the UK after ten years as a missionary in the 'third world.'

David, well used to making his confession to an elderly colleague, was taken quite unawares by the shrewdness of this dark haired rather untidy woman in her comfortable study with its

153

dark blue carpet and faded Persian rugs. At first he was cool and distinctly stand-offish but little by little he lowered his guard until he found himself speaking of events which he had thought to keep strictly to himself. He had not known how desperately he needed to talk, to unload the heavy burden of anger, guilt and frustration which had accumulated over the past 20 years. Suddenly, the hour was over and when Susie offered him an appointment at the same time the following week he had accepted it before he knew what he was doing.

The years of 'work' which David had done with Susie had quite simply changed his life. It had not, as he feared, caused him to leave religious life but had left him more than ever convinced that this was where he wanted to be. The insights gained during therapy had matured into a store of inner wisdom upon which he drew increasingly in his work as a priest.

When the therapy period ended, he and Susie became good friends and he stayed with her whenever his work brought him to the area. Now, with Katie as a solemn bequest from Robbie, he needed no other excuse to visit. His cigarette finished, David stood up, and, turning out his lights went down to join his small community at supper and their devotions for the vigil of the great feast of Christmas.

21

'Excuse me, Dr Walker,' Karen's voice was tentative. She knew how Chris hated being interrupted when he was with a client, but Dr Howard had been particularly insistent.

'Yes?' Chris was terse.

'I'm sorry, Doctor,' she said quickly, 'but it's Dr Howard and he said it's urgent.'

Chris sighed. 'It's all right, Karen,' he said, 'I'll come out.' Apologising briefly to the woman in the opposite chair, Chris left the room.

'Chris?' Michael Howard's voice was urgent. 'I'm sorry to interrupt you, but I've got a man of 40 who I think is a potential suicide risk. Is there any possibility that you could do an urgent domiciliary visit with me?'

Chris sighed to himself. Mike Howard had become exceptionally cautious about suicide risk in his patients since he had failed to recognise it in his own wife. While he would much rather that GPs were cautious than blasé about managing depressive illness, today was a particularly heavy day. Pulling himself together sharply, Chris said calmly, 'Of course, Mike. Let me look in the diary and we'll fix a time.'

Karen, at his elbow, held up the big office diary and pointed to one o'clock where a patient's name had been crossed out and the word cancelled scrawled across it. Chris glanced at the diary, nodded. 'How about one fifteen, Mike? Shall I meet you at the house?'

Michael acquiesced gratefully and, after Chris had returned to his client, dictated the patient's details and address to Karen.

Chris parked his car a few houses up the road from number 15 Chestnut Lane and picked up the packet of sandwiches which the thoughtful Karen had thrust into his hand as he left the clinic. Time was, he thought, when Rosie had made his sandwiches, but then that was when the children were small and before Rosie had gone back to her job as a social worker with the Mental Health

Team. She's too important to make my sandwiches now, thought Chris bitterly, realising at the same time that the knowledge that he was being completely unreasonable didn't make him feel any better.

What's gone wrong with our marriage, he thought? We used to be so happy. Even as he thought it, he knew that this was only partly true. In the very early days, he thought, they had been blissfully happy, but somehow, when Sam had been born, things had changed. At first, Rosie had had eyes only for the baby, and had thrown herself into the role of the perfect mother, reading all books on the attachment theory and child development.

Sam had not been an easy baby and Chris and Rosie had become progressively more exhausted as broken nights became the norm. They found it galling that two mental health professionals should be unable to pacify a small baby and Rosie had been especially angry with the health visitor whose advice she rejected out of hand. Looking back, it seemed to Chris that things had never really been right since then, although he found it impossible to put his finger on any specific reason for the insidious breakdown of their marriage. Chris had hoped that having another child would bring them closer together, and, for a couple of years that had indeed been the case. However, when their daughter, Virginia, was two years old, they had gone to spend a weekend with Chris's parents in Bristol. It had been a wonderful summer afternoon and Chris and his father had been left in charge of Sam and Ginny while the women went shopping. Chris had lain on his back on the lawn while the children romped around him like puppies, and then, overcome by the warmth of the sun and weariness from a night on call he had fallen asleep.

Chris felt sick as he replayed the events of that fatal afternoon to himself. He had been woken by four-year-old Sam screaming frantically and, sensing that something terrible was amiss he had run in the direction of the garden pond to find Ginny's body floating face down amongst the water lilies.

Chris knew that Rosie had never really forgiven him, and indeed he had never been able to forgive himself, but had learned to live with the pain of grief and guilt that had settled upon him that bright August afternoon. Rosie had refused point blank to have another child and poured upon Sam all the love and care that had once been shared out among her husband and family. When Sam was five, Rosie went back to work, full time, channelling her anger and grief into working with abused children and their families.

Chris, too, attempted to drown his pain in work and found himself coming home later and later as the years went by. He and Rosie continued to live together as man and wife, making love mechanically as if trying to prove to themselves that their marriage was intact when the reality was that they were more like colleagues sharing a house with a certain number of professional interests in common. When Sam was eight they decided to send him to boarding school and with no one to keep up appearances for, they lived their separate lives, leaving the house early and either returning late or going out again to evening meetings.

Now, Chris ate his sandwiches mechanically and wondered how it was that Michael Howard always managed to be late for appointments. At last Mike's red Volvo swung around the corner of the street and Chris got out to meet him.

John Carlisle sat gloomily at his kitchen table drinking coffee. The children's breakfast things were piled in a disordered heap on the draining board along with the previous night's supper dishes. John had not bothered about lunch. He wasn't really hungry and anyway there wasn't a lot in the fridge. He put his hand up to his face and felt the gritty stubble of his beard. I suppose I ought to shave before the doctor comes back he thought, but decided that he was too tired and lit a cigarette instead.

It was five months and twenty-five days since Mary's death, John calculated, and the pain was just as fierce as in those first terrible days after the funeral. At least I had some sense of her presence then, he thought, forgetting how devastating he had found it when he'd thought he had heard her feet on the gravel outside the house or the sound of her moving about in the bedroom overhead.

Terrible as those early days had been, John had been carried along by the momentum of events. There had been the funeral to arrange, the children to take care of and John had rallied to the task. He had asked for and received two week's compassionate leave to sort things out and had arranged for the children to stay with friends after school until he was able to pick them up.

The children had been good as gold and seemed to have adjusted to their new life. Everyone had told him that it was better not to talk too much to them about their mother. Let them remember her as she was, people said. They would get over it in no time. Children are very resilient. John 'knew' too that it was better to keep his grief to himself, to try to behave normally for the sake of the children. It wasn't fair, he thought, to burden them with his grief, so he had cried when he was on his own and kept up appearances as best he could with the children.

At first, the children had tried to talk about their mother. Jamie in particular had asked all sorts of penetrating and logical questions about death and funerals. He had wanted to know what happened to dead bodies when they were buried and how hot the furnace had to be to burn someone. On the day of the funeral Mary's sister, Julia, had heard Jamie's questions and, appalled, had taken him on one side and told him that he mustn't ask such terrible questions because they upset his daddy. Jamie, who had been trying to work out how Mummy could be in heaven if her body was burnt to a cinder didn't really understand why Julia was so angry and burst into tears, sobbing loudly 'I want my Mummy, I want my Mummy.'

Although she was a sixth form French teacher, Julia didn't understand small children very well, and began to feel guilty as well as distressed; at a loss for what to say next she fell back upon the wisdom of her generation which was that big boys don't cry. She told Jamie to pull himself together.

Jamie learned a lot from his Auntie Julia that day. He learned about the way grown-ups cope with death and that he must keep both his questions and his feelings to himself because they were equally unacceptable. After that the did his best to be a 'good boy' for his daddy and saved his tears for when he was in bed or alone with Oscar, his Teddy.

Lisa, who was 11, knew instinctively that talking about death was taboo. She kept out of Auntie Julia's way as much as she could and did her best to help her father. A motherly little girl by nature, she took over a lot of Jamie's care, sorting out his school clothes in the evening and making sure that he did his homework. When

Jamie had gone to bed she sat in her bedroom and brooded about the terrible thing that had befallen them all. She worried a good deal about her father who became thinner and more withdrawn as the weeks went by. Although he cooked supper for them every evening he never ate with them. At first Lisa believed him when he said that he had supper when the two of them were in bed, but there were only ever two dirty supper plates on the draining board in the morning, along with several empty coffee cups and a glass that smelled of whisky.

Sometimes Lisa would spend the night with her friend Francie, and she got to telling Francie's mum how much she missed her own mummy. About her worries concerning her father, however, she kept her own counsel, afraid that Mrs Mitchell would speak to him and betray her confidence.

John was lighting a new cigarette when the doorbell rang and sighing heavily, he stubbed it out and went to answer the door, wishing that everybody, including Dr Howard would just leave him alone and stop fussing. The doctor was accompanied by a tall blond-haired man whom Michael introduced as 'Dr Chris Walker, a colleague of mine.'

Chris smiled at John and offered him his hand. 'I'm sorry to intrude on you like this,' he said, 'but Dr Howard has suggested that it might be helpful for us to have a chat.

John opened his mouth to say that talking wouldn't bring Mary back but he thought better of it and invited the two men into the living room. Michael Howard looked quickly at Chris, 'would you rather . . .?' he began, and Chris nodded.

'John,' said Michael. 'I've got another visit to make nearby, so I'll leave you and Dr Walker to have a chat and I'll come back in a little while.'

John's living room was as messy as the kitchen, with empty coffee mugs on the hearth and an ashtray full of cigarette butts. John sat down on the sofa and looked at his hands while Chris pulled up a chair. For a moment or two there was silence, then Chris said gently, 'How long is it since your wife died, Mr Carlisle?'

'Five months,' said John, 'and twenty-five days,' his gaze still averted. Chris waited but John said nothing, the tears running slowly down his cheeks.

Chris's heart ached for the man as he remembered how he had felt after Ginny died. At last he said gently, 'Is it getting any easier?'

John shook his head. 'How can it be?' he said. 'She's gone. She won't come back. I've lost the only woman I've ever loved. How *can* it ever get easier?'

Chris waited silently, wondering how he should proceed when John suddenly found words to articulate his grief. It was as though Chris by his silence and evident compassion had provided the climatic conditions to precipitate the cloud of grief and despair that had hung over the bereaved man for so long. Chris sat, unprotected from the deluge, as John released the torrent of emotions that he'd bottled up for so long. Finally, he told the psychiatrist of how Mary had become confused and incontinent during the last week of her illness and of how he, John, had broken his promise to her that he would look after her at home until she died, by allowing Dr Howard and the Macmillan nurse to have her admitted to the hospital. The doctors and nurses, it seemed had been very kind but John had never forgiven himself for betraying his wife's trust in him.

When it seemed that the spate of grief had abated somewhat, Chris set about exploring whether or not John's depression was likely to lead him to take his own life. As he had suspected, John had no intention of committing suicide. True, he had often wished himself dead so that he could be with Mary, but he knew that to take his own life would be the ultimate betrayal of his promise to her to care for their children.

The door bell rang and, leaving John to recollect himself, Chris went to let Mike in. Chris led Mike into the kitchen and gave him a resumé of what had passed between John and himself.

Mike listened intently and, when Chris explained that he did not feel that John was likely to kill himself he heaved a sigh of relief.

'What about antidepressants?' he asked and Chris nodded.

'Yes,' he said, 'I was coming to that. I think that John needs both antidepressants and bereavement counselling. I suggest you start him on a sedative antidepressant so that he can get some sleep at night and I'll arrange for him to be seen on a regular basis until he has worked through his grief satisfactorily.'

Together the two doctors returned to the living room and Chris explained to John what they proposed. When John had agreed to come to the clinic the following week, Chris broadened the question of the children. Once more John hung his head.

'I *think* they're all right,' he said, 'but I never talk to them about their mother. I thought it was better not to remind them, that they'd get over it better if they were allowed to lead a normal life.'

Chris sighed. How difficult it is, he thought, and how we do fool ourselves about what children think and feel and understand. Gently, he explained to John that children of the ages of Jamie and Lisa experienced grief every bit as painfully as adults and that they also needed the opportunity to express their grief and be supported during the long months of bereavement. John looked down at the floor as Chris continued.

'You see, John, children have an added burden because although they grieve as deeply as adults they can easily misunderstand things. They can think, for example, that they have caused someone's death by being naughty or that their remaining parent will also die so that they will be left alone.'

John reached for his handkerchief and blew his nose.

Chris touched his knee gently. 'I'm sorry, John' he said. 'I'm not blaming you in the least, but it's important that you understand how Lisa and Jamie feel because *you* are the best person to help them.'

John nodded, 'It's all right,' he said. 'I do understand. Poor kids. No wonder they're so withdrawn and their school work's not as good as it should be.'

Chris looked at his watch. It was two o'clock. He stood up. 'Goodbye John, I'll leave you with Dr Howard now and and we'll meet again next week, but I'll be in touch with you about the counselling'

John made as if to get up but Chris smiled and and took his hand. 'I'll see myself out, John . . . goodbye,' and turning, he left the two men on their own.

It was nearly nine when Chris got home that night to find that

Rosie had gone out, leaving a blue envelope with his name on in the middle of the kitchen table.

Wearily, he sat down and, tearing open the envelope pulled out the letter and opened it out to read.

Dear Chris,

I'm going away for a few days to think things over. I'm tired of pretending that everything is fine between us, and (here the writing was less easy to decipher) and, (he read), I have found someone else. I'm really sorry. I'll be in touch in a few days when I've worked out what to do. Rosie.

22

'My name is Jamie', said the boy with the fair hair to the other children in the bereavement group, 'and I'm going to be eight next Thursday.'

The social worker smiled at him. 'Thank you, Jamie, she said. 'Would you like to tell us about your mum or would you rather wait a bit?'

Jamie bit his lip. 'My mum died six month's ago . . .' he said quickly. The tears he'd tried so hard to keep at bay ran down his cheeks and fell silently on to his new blue sweatshirt. He tired to go on but the words wouldn't come. As he sat there struggling to control himself, Jamie felt his sister Lisa's warm hand insinuate itself into his and he gave it a grateful squeeze.

Jamie gulped. 'I'm all right,' he said. 'I can go on now.'

'Are you sure Jamie?' Cathy's voice was low and tender.

'Yes. I'm sure. What do you want me to say?'

'Could you tell us how it began, Jamie? When did you first know that your mother was ill?'

'They didn't tell us at first,' said Jamie. 'But we knew. Lisa and I always knew when there was something wrong. We could tell by their voices, by the way they looked. We just knew.'

'What did you think was happening, Jamie?'

'Well, we didn't know exactly. We just knew something was wrong.'

Now it was Lisa's turn to cry. 'We thought they'd had a row. Mum had been crying. She looked absolutely awful. We were scared. We'd never seen them look like that before.'

Jamie held Lisa's hand tightly.

'It was ages before they told us anything,' she said. 'It was really horrible not knowing what was going on. We'd come into the room and they'd stop talking. They'd go into the bedroom and shut the door and we could hear Mum crying.

We thought, we thought . . .' Jamie interrupted his sister.

'What did you think, Jamie?' Cathy's voice was quietly encouraging.

163

Jamie gave a strangled sob. 'We thought they were going to get divorced. We thought Dad wanted to leave home and that's why Mum was always crying.'

Cathy looked at Lisa. 'How did you feel about it, Lisa?'

Lisa spoke quietly. 'I wish they'd told us right from the beginning. It wouldn't have been so bad if we'd known. Once they did tell us, we could help look after Mum when she was sad.'

'At least we knew then it wasn't *our* fault she was crying.' Jamie was angry now.

Cathy smiled at the two children. 'Jamie, Lisa,' she said, 'thank you very much. You've been very brave, talking about things which are so painful. I'm sure it's really helpful for the others, too.'

The other children in the group nodded and Alice spoke up. 'It was just the same with my Dad,' she said. 'They didn't even tell me he was dying so I never said goodbye to him, or thank you or anything.'

'You're right Alice, it's not fair, but,' said Cathy gently, 'you see, sometimes grown-ups don't understand how children think. They forget how it was when *they* were children. They're trying to protect you and the sad thing is, they make things much worse.'

'Someone should tell them, then.' Alice was still angry. 'Why don't the doctors tell them?'

'Sometimes even the doctors don't understand, Alice. They think that children don't understand about illness and death and that it's better to protect them from all the sadness.'

'But we *do* know about illness and dying.' Alice was outraged. 'Our dog died because he got cancer.'

'And our cat was run over, when I was six,' said William. 'I remember burying her in the garden when she died.'

'Grown ups are wrong about death,' said Alice. I was so sad when my Dad was ill, but I couldn't talk about it because it was all a big secret. I wish they'd told me. I'll always feel bad that I never said goodbye.'

Rosie Walker looked up from her desk when Cathy came into the social work office and made a beeline for the kettle. 'How'd it go?'

'Oh, fine thanks, but it always churns me up a bit. Kids break

164

through one's defences. They're so truthful. They've no guile. It makes me want to weep, the way some of them have suffered. There was a new pair in the group this afternoon, a brother and sister whose mother died of breast cancer six months ago. They were sent up because the school was concerned about them.'

'What's the story, then?' said Rosie. 'Do you want to talk about it?'

'Oh, it's the same old story. The parents wanted to protect them so they didn't tell them what was wrong with their mother for a while.'

'And the kids picked up the vibes?'

'Yes, poor little devils. They thought the parents were quarrelling, thought they were heading for divorce.'

If the mention of divorce caused Rosie pain, she gave no sign. 'Did the children think it was their fault?' she said.

'Of course. Kids seem to be programmed to take on the guilt of the world. They remembered a time when they'd been naughty and the parents had a difference of opinion about it, and they jumped to the conclusion that they had caused a rift. They were heartbroken. Thought they'd have to go into care.'

'O God! And what about when she was terminal?'

'We haven't got that far yet. They're only starting to admit their anger about the early stages of their mother's illness.'

'When do you see them again?'

'Next week. I'm seeing the group weekly for six sessions and then I'll assess where we've got to.'

'What about the father? Are you seeing him too?'

'Oh, yes. He needs as much help as they do. Not only is he still devastated by his wife's death, but now he has the added guilt of the children's distress. He believed the old myth that kids are resilient – that they get over bereavement without it really affecting them.

'You mean he didn't notice they were grieving?'

'Not really. He was so caught up in his own grief and so determined not to let them see him cry that he deceived himself. He was "brave" for the children and they didn't want to let him down.'

'What about the GP. Didn't he keep an eye on the family?'

'Not really. I don't think he really understands a lot about bereavement himself and, anyway, he's run off his feet. He doesn't really have the energy to be proactive. He can only deal with the problems that turn upon his doorstep.'

'Which leaves *us*?'

'That's about it. And we're only beginning to get a grip on things. Think of all the children whose parents are divorced. What about *their* grief?'

'Come on, Cathy. You can only do what you can do. How's the camp project coming along?'

'It's fixed for July. There are 20 children booked in and ten in the adult group. We're modelling it on the "Winston's Wish" programme that Julie Stokes is running in Gloucester.'

'Winston's Wish?'

'Winston's a teddy bear: an amazing, wise, mythical teddy bear who understands about grief in children. Julie and her team use him as a way of communicating with the bereaved children they work with and they run a "Camp Winston" where they bring children together over a weekend. They let them talk about their loss, play, draw and so on.

'Sounds amazing,' said Rosie, thinking of young Sam's distress at her recent separation from Chris.

There's a candle lighting service and they have a sort of project book where they record their important memories. They all get a Winston sweatshirt and, at the end, a Winston bear.'

'What about the parents?'

'They have their own meeting and then on the Sunday afternoon the parents and the children come together again.'

'Sounds really good. Will the youngsters you saw today be coming?'

'I hope so,' said Cathy. She was silent for a moment, then looking at her watch stood up abruptly. 'Well, no rest for the wicked. I've got another client coming soon.'

Rosie's brow furrowed. 'Don't over do it,' she said, but Cathy was already out of the door.

23

New Year's Day was one of Susie's favourite days. She loved the feeling of new beginnings, the excitement of an empty year spread out in front of her, of wondering what the unfurling days would bring. She listened to the sound of Ben gently moving round the kitchen and thought how lucky she was to love and be loved by such a good and gentle man. It had not always been so. Susie's first marriage had been a disaster and it had taken her many years to work through the complex emotions which had emerged during the early years of her own therapy. She laughed when she thought how so many of her friends and clients thought that she had always been wise and calm as she was now. Therapists aren't born, she would say, they are forged like steel in a furnace. After all, if I hadn't been in a mess myself, how on earth would I know what to say to you?

At one-thirty precisely, the door bell rang. 'That'll be Katie,' said David. 'Shall I let her in?'

'Would you? Thanks,' said Susie vaguely as she pored over her old diary trying to decide which telephone numbers needed to be transferred into the new one.

'David!' Katie exclaimed, nearly dropping the large white azalea which she had bought for Susie. 'I didn't know you were going to be here!'

David grinned. 'I didn't know myself, until yesterday. But when Susie told me that you were coming to lunch, I decided that it was too good an opportunity to miss.'

'Hi,' said Susie, 'come along in.'

'Ben,' she called. 'Katie's here. Are we ready?'

Ben, who enjoyed cooking, grinned at his wife's use of the royal 'we' and answered in the affirmative.

'Well!' said Susie, as she settled back on the sofa with her coffee, 'how's it going, Katie?'

Taking a small bite out of her Belgian chocolate so that it would last longer, Katie smiled and said, 'Well, believe it or not, I'm loving it.'

'What sort of ward are you on now?' asked David, barely able to conceal his delight that Katie's new life as a student nurse was turning out to be such a success.

'I'm on male surgical at the moment,' said Katie. 'Lots of appendixes and a fair bit of cancer.'

'How are you coping with the cancer patients,' said David, aware that it was less than three years since Robbie's death.

Katie was sober. 'Fine, really,' she said. 'It makes me think of him, of course, but then I think about him a lot anyway. It makes me long for the day when I know enough to be of use to the patients. You know,' she paused, 'when I know what to say to them, how to comfort them, the way you and Susie do.'

David smiled at Katie's earnest face. 'One step at a time,' he said, 'and don't underestimate the value of just being yourself. It's not the clever words that matter most, it's the love that you put into it, the warmth of the way you relate to people without even realising it.'

They sat for a while in silence, until Susie stretched and said, 'Well, folks, how about a walk in the park?'

New Year's Day was Sam Walker's birthday and this year, his fourteenth, he was spending part of the day with his father before returning for an evening party at his home where he lived with his mother. As they walked together across the park towards the frozen pond, Sam looked across at his father.

'What did you do last night, Dad,' he asked. 'Did you see the New Year in?'

Chris smiled and put his arm around his son's shoulders. Sam was always solicitous for him, worried about him being on his own.

'I had a whisky, Sam,' he said, 'and I drank to the hope of a happier year for all of us.'

'Does that mean . . .' Sam's voice died away as he became tongue tied. 'Is there any chance . . .' he began again.

Chris, knowing what his son was trying to say, said quietly, 'If you're asking whether Mum and I will be getting back together again, Sam, I'm afraid that the answer is no.'

Sam was silent for a while ... 'Dad,' he said, 'do you miss Mum? Are you lonely?'

Chris walked on slowly while he tried to work out the best way to answer his son's question. How could you explain to a 14 year old about the death of a marriage? How could you tell your son that you no longer loved his mother?

'It's okay, Sam,' he said. 'Really ... Most of the time I'm too busy to be lonely,' he paused, and his inner voice told him that Sam deserved a more honest answer than this. He took a deep breath and began slowly: 'I suppose, to be truthful,' he said, 'I *am* lonely. It's not that I miss your mum so much as that I miss having someone with whom to share my life. It can be a bit lonely coming back to an empty house at night, and, the weekends can be a bit bleak if you're not around.'

Sam put his arm through his father's and gave it a sort of squeeze, then, embarrassed lest anyone see him, said, 'race you to the pond, Dad,' and began to run, his skates clattering noisily together as he moved.

Chris was concentrating so hard on trying to catch Sam that he almost missed Susie and Ben, David and Katie as they walked along the path that led to the pond.

'Hey, doctor, watch it,' said Susie, grinning at Chris as he struggled to regain his breath. 'Are you training for the marathon or something?'

Chris laughed, delighted to see his friend and mentor. 'No,' he said, 'I'm trying, rather foolishly, to keep up with a 14 year old. What brings you out of hibernation? I thought you stayed indoors all winter?'

'Sh, sh,' said Susie. 'I'm trying to impress my guests ... Chris, have you met David Meredith?'

Chris shook hands with the tall Jesuit and, as Susie introduced him to Katie Chris said, 'Hello, Katie. I hardly recognised you, how are you?'

Katie smiled shyly. 'I'm very well,' she said, 'thank you.'

If Susie was surprised, she made no comment, but said, 'Why don't you and Sam come and have some tea with us when you've finished skating? We've got enough Christmas cake and mince pies left to feed a legion.'

169

'I'll have to ask Sam,' said Chris. 'It's his birthday today. Can we leave it open, Susie? I'd love to, but . . .'

Sam appeared, suddenly from behind a tree. 'Hello, Mrs Wellington,' he said politely. 'Happy New Year.'

'Happy birthday, Sam,' said Susie. 'How would you like to come to tea when you've finished skating?'

Sam looked at Chris, and then, looking back at Susie said, 'Thank you very much. We'd love to.' Then running to his father he said, 'Come on, Dad, the ice is quite safe. I've tested it and it's wonderful.'

Susie pushed back her sleeve to check her watch, 'See you in an hour,' she said, and tucking her arm through her husband's she said, 'Come on, Ben, I'm getting cold.

'Dad!' John Carlisle looked up from his newspaper. 'Yes, Jamie,' he said.

'Dad,' Jamie paused, 'do you think the ice on the pond is strong enough to skate on yet?'

John looked out of the window and saw that the lawn was still white with frost.

'I don't know, Jamie,' he said. 'Do you want to go and find out?'

'Oh Dad! Could we?' Jamie's face shone with pleasure.

'Go and ask Lisa and Alice,' said John, 'and see what they want to do!'

Jamie rushed out of the room and John heard him calling as he bounded up the stairs. 'Lisa! Dad says we can go skating. Do you want to go?'

Lisa looked up from the magazine that she and her friend Alice were reading, and, feigning indifference, said, 'What do you think Al?' Do you want to go skating?'

Alice, who at just 13, was six months younger than her friend, felt no need to be superior and said at once. 'Great. Do let's. We can pick up my skates on the way to the park.'

'Why don't you come back here for tea?' said Harriet to John as the children piled back into the car. 'I'll have finished sewing by then and it'll be good to have some company.'

John smiled. 'Thanks, Harriet,' he said, 'I'd like that.'

John stamped his feet to keep warm as he watched the children skate and wondered if it was worth buying a pair of skates for himself. How Mary would have enjoyed seeing this he thought, as Lisa glided by, arm in arm with Alice. She'd have liked Harriet too he mused, but, of course, *he* would never have met Harriet if Mary hadn't died, his inner demon told him and, momentarily his peace evaporated and the colourful figures on the lake seemed no more than grey shadows.

John shook himself. Shut up, he said to the voice, and once again the figures glowed in the pale wintry sunshine. His gaze scanned the scene on the lake and then moved idly to the path until he saw a face that he recognised. It was Chris Walker, the psychiatrist whom he had seen when he was so depressed after Mary's death.

John was tempted to walk over and greet him, but thought better of it. Poor man, he thought. Leave him be. He's off duty and needs time to himself like anyone else.

Had Chris been aware of John's thoughts he would have been grateful, although he had little problem these days with encountering patients out of hours. The issue of boundaries between work and time off had been a major issue in his brief therapeutic contract with Susie after Rosie had left him. Poor as their relationship had been, it had simply never occurred to Chris that his wife would leave him and it had taken him some time to accept that he was as much 'to blame' as she was. Not that Susie had ever talked to him in terms of blame – that was certainly not her way. She had, however, helped Chris to see the marriage from Rosie's point of view and how he had unconsciously put his work before his relationship with his wife and son.

'Oh God,' Chris had said morosely, 'is there nothing new under the sun? Do you realise that I am repeating the mistakes that my father made in his relationship with my mother?'

Susie had just grinned. 'Are you surprised? Don't you realise that we all do it? At least you've realised it, which was more than your father did!'

Gradually Chris had become accustomed to his celibate life. When the decree absolute came through he had thought, fleetingly, that he was free to marry again, but he made no conscious effort to find a new partner. At 43, Chris relaxed into his bachelor existence and told himself that he was happier than he had been for years.

It came as something of a surprise, therefore, to find himself admiring Katie's wild red hair and long slender legs as he faced her across Susie's drawing room when they all went back there for tea. Briefly distracted by wondering what she would look like without the forest green sweater and black trousers, he lost the thread of the conversation and had to pull himself sharply together.

'Dr Walker?'

Chris looked up from his desk. 'Hello, Karen,' he said. 'I thought you'd gone home.'

Karen smiled her usual polite enigmatic smile. 'I was just going,' she said, 'when the phone rang. It's the hospital. There's an overdose on Jenner Ward that they'd like you to see tonight.'

Chris sighed. 'What did you say?' he said wearily.

'I said you'd ring them back,' she said. 'The houseman did sound a bit anxious.'

Chris grinned. 'Okay,' he said. 'Give me the number. I'll ring them in a minute or two, I promise.'

'Thank you doctor,' said his secretary. 'I'm off now. Good night.'

It was gone eight o'clock by the time Chris pushed open the double doors that led to Jenner Ward. As he walked down the ward towards the nurses station Chris became aware of a mop of flame-coloured hair only moderately successfully anchored to its owner's head by a motley of pins and a large tortoiseshell clip.

'Hello,' said the owner of the hair, 'have you come to see Wendy Hughes?' It was a moment or two before Chris found his tongue. 'Wendy?' he said, looking down at the piece of paper which Karen had given him. 'Ah, yes, Wendy Hughes.'

Smiling, Katie handed him a set of notes.

'Hello, Katie!' he said. 'I didn't expect to find you here!'

Katie smiled and Chris saw that her eyes were a wonderful green colour.

'I'm in my third year, now,' she said. 'They've even left me in charge while the staff nurse has her coffee break!'

Chris grinned. 'Are you sure you can manage?' he said.

Katie feigned a furtive look. 'Sometimes I think I'm only

pretending to be a nurse,' she said, 'and they're sure to find me out sooner or later!'

'Don't tell anyone,' said Chris, 'but I quite often feel the same!'

Katie felt a powerful urge to put her arms around the tall psychiatrist's neck and kiss him, but she restrained herself and, seeing one of the other nurses approaching, she said. 'Would you like to see Mrs Hughes in Sister's office, doctor?'

It took Chris nearly an hour to see Mrs Hughes, who was an unhappy young woman who had decided to take an overdose of paracetamol because her husband was having an affair with another woman. When he had finished he looked in vain for Katie but the careworn day shift had been replaced by a bustling threesome of older women who were busily tidying beds and handing out night sedation and laxatives. Katie, he realised, had gone home.

24

'Charlotte! For Pete's sake, will you turn the volume down a bit!' Charlotte Holmes stuck her head out of her bedroom door. 'Sorry, Mum,' she said, 'what did you say?'

Jessica grinned up at her daughter standing above her on the landing. 'I said please could you turn the music down a bit,' she said. 'Tom and I can't hear ourselves think.'

'Oh, sorry,' said Charlotte and disappeared back into her bedroom where her three friends Alice, Lisa and Emma were sprawled on the floor reading magazines.

'Too loud?' asked Lisa, grinning and pointing to the ghetto blaster beside her.

Charlotte nodded. 'Sorry,' she said. 'The walls are a bit thin.'

'Do you think they'll ever get married?' said Emma.

'I don't know,' said Charlotte. 'I think they're happy just as they are. What about your mum?'

Emma was thoughtful. 'I reckon they'll get married when Mum finishes her training,' she said. 'I suppose they're just making sure that they're really suited. Mum hasn't had much luck with men up till now.'

But Chris is different, isn't he?' said Alice. 'After all, he's a doctor.'

'I don't see what difference being a doctor makes. I think Mum's right to be wary,' said Emma sharply. 'She just wants to be sure, for all our sakes, and,' she paused, 'because of Robbie.'

'Who's Robbie,' asked Lisa, who hadn't known Emma as long as she'd known Alice.

'He was a friend of Mum's who died.' said Emma. 'He left us his flat and some money. He and Mum met while they were both in hospital.'

'Why did he die?' said Lisa, who knew quite a bit about illness and death.

'He had leukaemia,' said Emma. 'They only knew each other about ten days.'

'God! How romantic,' said Lisa. 'And he left you his flat? It's like a fairy story.'

'It is a bit,' said Emma, 'but it happens to be true.'

'David,' said Katie, as they stood and watched the ducks playing on the pond. 'Do you think that Robbie would want me to marry Chris?'

'It's not what Robbie wants, Katie, but what *you* want,' said David quietly. 'Do *you* want to marry him?'

Katie smiled. 'Yes,' she said, 'I suppose I'm a bit scared. I've never been very lucky in my relationships and I'm terrified of hurting and being hurt all over again.

'Shall we sit down for a bit?' said David, as they approached a bench. 'I could do with a breather.' David rolled his cigarette while he thought. 'Have you talked to Susie about this?' he said a last.

'Oh yes,' said Katie. 'She thinks we'll be fine. She says that Chris and I are both much more mature now and that we've a good chance of making a go of it.'

'What about the children?' said David. 'How do they feel?'

Katie laughed. 'Oh, they're all for it,' she said. They adore Chris – and Emma and Sam are as thick as thieves.'

'Well,' said David, 'What more do you want?'

'You,' said Katie urgently. 'I want you to marry us!'

'Oh, my Lord,' said David, grinning, 'you'll get me excommunicated yet, Katie Roberts!'

'Daddy,' said little Lizzie solemnly, looking up from Mrs Mog, the rather battered doll which she was examining with a bright red plastic stethoscope.

'Yes,' said Michael. 'What can I do for you, nurse?'

'I'm not a nurse,' said his daughter crossly. 'I'm a doctor!'

'Oops! Sorry,' Michael grinned at his wife as she entered the room.

'How can I help you, *Doctor* Howard?' he said solemnly.

'Daddy,' said Lizzie, climbing up on to his knee, 'Andrew says that Mrs Mog has got cancer and she's going to die.'

Michael looked into his little daughter's eyes as they filled with tears.

'No, darling,' he said. 'Andrew's got it wrong. Just because she's got cancer doesn't mean that Mrs Mog's going to die. Lots and lots of people get better from cancer and I'm sure Mrs Mog will be just fine.'

Lizzie smiled, and kissing her father wetly on the cheek, returned to her patient's bedside.

Jane bent over the back of her husbands chair and kissed him gently on the bald patch which had recently appeared in the middle of his head. 'Michael,' she whispered, 'I love you.'

Susie always got slightly tipsy at weddings and Katie's wedding, five year after Robbie's death, was no exception. Both Chris and Katie had wanted it to be a quiet family affair so Susie had offered to host the reception at her house. 'After all, Katie,' she had said, 'didn't I adopt you as a daughter the very first night we met?'

Katie smiled and gave Susie a hug while her mind went back to that warm summer evening when she and Robbie had lain side by side on a rug at the end of the garden.

'Dearest Susie,' she said. 'I owe you so much, you and Ben and David and . . .' she paused, 'and Robbie.'

'Nonsense,' said Susie, gruffly. 'All we did was clear the ground a bit, give you the space to grow.'

While Chris and Katie Walker, on their honeymoon at last, watched the sun go down behind the dome of the Church of Santa Maria del Salute in Venice, John Carlisle and his wife Harriet were drinking tea at their kitchen table, mulling over their respective days. Meanwhile, psychotherapist Susie Wellington was listening intently to a weeping client, while Father David Meredith sat at his desk 60 miles away, smoking a cigarette and trying to decide which of a pile of letters he should answer next.

Michael Howard, as was his custom at six in the evening, was sitting in his surgery listening to one of his patients, while Social Worker Sarah Jane Westward was sitting wearily at her computer terminal in the hospital wishing that her managers did not require quite such a detailed account of her stewardship.

Lisa and Jamie, Emma and her younger siblings and Alice, Charlotte and Sam were all doing their homework, while somewhere in the city, invisible to the majority of its citizens, Macmillan

Nurse Victoria Woodhouse was driving home thinking about a young woman who was dying of cancer and wondering how the hell the husband would cope on his own with three young children.

APPENDIX

Comments on Chapters

Comment on Chapter 1

In which Mary Carlisle discovers that she has breast cancer

The terror which many people experience when they first suspect that they have cancer is often endured in secret as they either attempt to deny its existence or try to protect their relatives from distress. Allowing a person to tell their story and recount their feelings is an integral part of therapy. Adults, like children, when they are frightened or ill, need a *secure base*, a person who will 'be there' for them, listen to them and accept their feelings. This role of attachment figure is usually fulfilled by a parent, spouse or close friend, but in the absence of these, a professional carer should be able either to give support or facilitate communication with a friend or relative of the patient.

Mary's consultation with her doctor is very unsatisfactory, not because he does not care but because he is too harassed and short of time to give her the attention she needs. He has given her adequate physical care but has not met her needs to ventilate her emotions, to be supported, to ask questions and receive information at a pace and in a language that she can absorb.

We owe our understanding of the importance of a secure base, a parent or parent figure who will be there for the small child when he or she is tired, ill or frightened, to Dr John Bowlby, a British psychiatrist who worked at the Tavistock Clinic in London. That adults have precisely the same attachment needs as children when they are distressed is much less widely known.

Comment on Chapter 2

In which Mary talks to Nurse Caroline

Mary's interview with Caroline illustrates the healing potential of the *safe space*. The safe space is created by a relationship in which a person feels sufficiently accepted and secure to talk through issues which cause them fear, embarrassment or shame. It can be a relationship between partners, between parent and child, health care worker and patient, therapist and client, priest and penitent, and so on. Psychotherapist Carl Rogers has listed what he sees as the core conditions for such a therapeutic encounter: congruence, empathy and unconditional positive regard.

Congruence. Being consistent and in agreement means that the person in the therapeutic role does not act a role, put on a façade but is relatively transparent and remains his or her 'self'. The importance of congruence will perhaps become clearer if we consider how difficult it is to trust and feel comfortable with someone who puts on a professional façade, a 'mask' so that we cannot tell what they are really thinking about us. The wearing of such masks in medicine is far less frequent than it was in the days of the consultant surgeon or physicians who expected to be treated as if they were God. Today's doctors and nurses are, mostly, more human and more approachable. There is always, however, the temptation to retreat behind a protective, somewhat distant, façade because we feel much less vulnerable to the pain of the patient.

Empathy. Empathy is the ability to enter into the patient's world and feel it as if it was our own. It is important, however, that we never lose sight of the phrase 'as if', because in that lies our protection from being overwhelmed by the pain of the other.

Unconditional positive regard. This means that the therapist (parent, doctor, or whoever) accepts the client unconditionally, that is without imposing conditions. It is not a case of 'I will accept you *if* . . . but 'my acceptance of you is not dependent upon your good behaviour, politeness, compliance, etc.' It is impossible to exaggerate the importance of this unconditional acceptance, especially for those oppressed and frightened people who automatically expect to be judged and rejected as being not good enough.

The *safe space* in which the person is understood and is accepted unconditionally is the adult equivalent of the young child's *secure base*. A patient who has no *confiding tie*, no one to listen empathically and accept unconditionally is very much vulnerable to anxiety and depression than one who is well supported. This human need for support and the ways in which it may be met is at the root of the development of the various support programmes which are enriching the care of cancer patients and their families.

Comment on Chapter 3

In which Mary Carlisle tells her husband John about the lump in her breast

It is absurdly easy for busy doctors who see a patient on their own to forget that 'no man is an island,' (John Donne) and that the majority of people have close relations and friends who will not only be affected by the patient's illness but will also affect how the patient copes with his or her illness. The main problem is one of time – it can take twice as long to see a patient and then his or her relative. Why then do we not interview them together? Some doctors, of course, do this. Sometimes, I do myself, but I find, especially at a first meeting that it is much easier for me to establish a good rapport with a patient if I see him or her on their own. It is quite common for a patient's spouse to answer the doctor's questions for the patient, so that information gathering is quite difficult. If the couple have a close relationship they will frequently try to protect the other, either by playing down their symptoms or by trying to prevent the doctor from answering the patient's questions frankly.

It is important to remember, too, that not all marriages are made in heaven and there may be considerable animosity between spouses, perhaps even fear. One of my patient's husbands threw her wig (she had lost her hair because of chemotherapy) across the room.

John, Mary's husband, is clearly very loving and a tower of strength. Once she has told him of her fears he is able to function as her secure base, the attachment figure to whom she can turn in her fear and grief. If John had not been so supportive or if Mary had been on her own, she would have needed support from friends or outside her immediate circle.

Ideally, then, the doctor must see the patient on his or her own and then the relative who, because he or she is so deeply affected by what is happening to his or her spouse is almost a 'patient' in his or her own right.

Comment on Chapter 4

In which Katie learns that she has cancer and Sarah and Caroline have supervision with psychiatrist Chris Walker

Katie's brief meeting with gynaecologist Peter Smith is as 'good' as it can be given the time constraints of a busy out patient department and Peter's lack of counselling skills. Although we do not eavesdrop on Katie's interview with Clare, the Oncology Support Nurse, it will be similar to Mary's interview with Caroline. The two interviews illustrate the need that patients have for time and support while they process 'bad news' and the way in which two different health professionals can work together for the benefit of the patient.

Katie's situation differs radically from Mary's in that she has no partner to support her and no one to care for her children while she is in hospital. Not only does Katie have logistical problems about care for her three children, she has the added burden of a difficult adolescent who is putting herself at risk of pregnancy, venereal disease and AIDS. These complex issues may not be part of Katie's surgical problem but they have to be addressed if Katie is to be free to undergo physical treatment for her cancer, let alone treatment for herself as a whole individual.

It may seem excessive to have added in the burden of sexual abuse in both mother and daughter, but in 'real life' physical, financial and emotional problems are interlocked so that it takes carers from a number of different disciplines to resolve them. It is only when professionals are prepared to acknowledge each other's differing expertise that 'holistic' care can be delivered. This is what *multidisciplinary team work* is about.

Comment on Chapter 5

In which Doctor Michael Howard's wife Jane is revealed to be 'clinically' depressed

In an ideal world all doctors would be gentle and sensitive with all their patients, especially those who are very distressed or have serious problems. They would function fully as professionals, alert for problems and clues to a diagnosis while at the same time being warm and human, empathic and understanding. In their private lives they would be loving and attentive to their spouses and children, spending time with them, listening to their problems with all the love and skill they lavished upon their patients. Real life, however, is just not like that.

First of all, in most GP's surgeries, each patient is allocated about ten minutes with the doctor. This means that the doctor has only ten minutes in which to disengage his mind from the previous patient and tune in to the new person and find out what his or her problems are. First and foremost, the doctor is on the alert for serious, treatable disease. If he misses something like cancer, a heart condition or diabetes the patient may become very ill or even die. Although it is right that doctors prioritise in this way, it means the patient's emotional needs inevitably take second place to their physical ones. If the person has a family member or a good friend to support them, their needs will be at least partially met, but if the patient has no 'confiding tie' then they may suffer quite unnecessarily loneliness and anxiety.

In this chapter I have tried to show how a doctor's family can miss out on the support they need because he is preoccupied with his work (or, as we shall see later, with other things.) Jane, Michael's wife, is caught up in a vicious circle of events: the loss of the excitement, friendship and sense of worth which she had in her job which she gave up to have a family; the sleep disturbance and increasing fatigue that accompany a depressive illness; a diminished sense of personal worth which makes her feel useless and unattractive so that she feels unable to make an effort to maintain her friendships and social life.

Her GP rightly enquires directly if she has thought of taking her life and finds that not only has she thought of doing this but has actually considered *how* she might do it. She is clearly at risk of killing herself and needs urgent supervision and antidepressant medication. In these circumstances the doctor might have to section her, or detain her in a place of safety, if necessary against her will, under the section of the Mental Health Act relating to persons at risk to themselves or others. This is one of the very few situations in which the doctor must override his patient's wishes for their own safety.

Comment on Chapter 6

In which Katie's 13–year-old daughter, Emma, talks to psychiatrist Chris Walker about her relationships with her father and her boyfriend

In this chapter we see how, by treating her sensitively and honestly, Chris wins Emma's confidence so that she talks openly about her experience with her father when she was a small girl and her present relationship with her boyfriend, Joe. The scenario depicted, in which Emma's story of abuse by her father was not believed by her mother is unfortunately very common. A mother finds it almost impossible to believe that the man she loves could do anything so monstrous, and, when he denies it she prefers to believe him rather than the child.

Emma is lucky that her abuse has come to light when she is only 13, for at least she can now be given help to reduce the long term effects of such a traumatic event. Many people have a very different experience. Some carry the memory of abuse as a dark secret which they do not feel able to reveal because of the sense of shame it engenders. It is a sad paradox that abused children usually feel guilty that they have been abused, that there must be something wrong with *them*, rather than the person who abused them.

In a small minority of people the memory of the abuse is so terrible that their unconscious mind represses it, locks it away, so that they forget that it ever happened. If this was the end of it all, there would be no problem, but the buried memory affects the person in their relationships throughout their life. They may, for example, be quite unable to make healthy relationships with persons of the opposite sex, or they may be afraid of physical contact or intimacy.

The shame they felt at the time of the episode, although not accessible to the conscious memory affects the way they feel about themselves and lowers their sense of personal self-worth. These memories may surface unexpectedly or during the course of therapy in later life. Only then, when these issues are faced openly and the memories explored, is healing possible.

Some women are affected differently by the memory of abuse in that, because of their experience, they tend to sexualise relationships. They confuse love with sex and, because they don't know how to say no, they become extremely vulnerable to be taken advantage of by unscrupulous men.

In this way, the woman who was a victim in childhood continues to be a victim in adolescence and adult life. Emma, who is having sex with Joe without really wanting to, but because she doesn't know how to say no, would come into this category.

Comment on Chapter 7

In which psychiatrist Chris Walker talks to GP Michael Howard about the latter's relationship with his wife Jane

Jane's depression is not an out of the blue affair – an endogenous depression – but is a reaction to her life situation and the way in which her husband has, quite unwittingly, been insensitive to her needs.

As to Michael's brief infidelity, the reader may judge harshly or feel that it is not for them to cast the first stone. The important point to draw from this chapter is the way the psychiatrist handles Michael, non-judgmentally but pointing out to him the consequences of his actions. Michael, like his patient Mary, needs a 'safe space' in which to admit his weakness and acknowledge his shame.

The other point to be taken from this chapter is the vulnerability of all the healers. Michael, who may seem all wise and all powerful (on a good day!) to some of his patients, is in reality a very mixed-up man who has put his family life and even his wife's life at risk by his preoccupation with himself, his work and his sexual fantasies.

Chris, the psychiatrist, who is clearly wiser than Mike, has his own vulnerabilities and needs Susie's help to cope with them and to grow as a therapist and a man. Susie's own vulnerabilities remain, in this story, hidden but we may be quite sure that she has them. We are all like sets of Russian Dolls, people within people, within people. The great therapeutic joke, of course, is encapsulated in Jung's quotation: 'Only the wounded healer can heal.'

Comment on Chapter 8

In which Katie Roberts meets psychiatrist Chris Walker and talks about her feelings about being abused by her father

It may seem to some readers that I have dwelt excessively on child abuse by portraying both Emma and her mother Katie as 'victims'. Statistically, this may be true but I have clear memories of some of the young women with cervical cancer that I have cared for over the years and Katie is a composite of them all. My memory is of bright, vulnerable young women who, for whatever reason, began to have intercourse in their mid teens and then went on to a series of unstable relationships. I remember, too, that many of these women had difficult teenage daughters, some of whom were promiscuous, and that there was frequently difficulty about who should have custody of the children when the women died. I have vivid memories of frightened women who thought they could 'bequeath' their children like property to their sisters or some trusted relatives because they did not want them to go to the children's fathers most of whom had new partners.

Sorting out this kind of social and emotional mess is the daily task of hospice multidisciplinary teams. 'No man is an island' and any young woman dying of cancer has an intricate network of relationships: parents, siblings, partners, ex-partners, children and friends, all of whom will be profoundly affected by her death. A death, particularly an 'untimely' death is like a stone dropped in a pond; there are ripples which spread wide into the community, touching the lives of many. A 'bad' death, one in which the patient's symptoms are uncontrolled and their emotional needs not met, sends bad ripples into the community, messages that cancer is terrible, that death is a disaster and that no one really cares about the sick and the dying. A 'good' death, on the other hand, in which symptoms are well controlled, emotional needs met, and the patient or his or her 'significant others' lovingly cared for, sends good ripples; messages that pain can be controlled, that frightened, angry people are heard and comforted and that death, whilst sad, need not necessarily be a disaster. Such good messages affect the whole community, diminishing the level of fear of cancer and encouraging people to seek help earlier so that they have a better chance of cure or worthwhile palliation.

The hospice movement, or rather the palliative care movement (for skilled care of the dying is now also an accepted part of hospital services) has therefore a 'prophetic' role to the rest of medicine, acknowledging as it does, the need for holistic, whole-person care of sick people in general and the dying in particular.

Comment on Chapter 9

In which Mary meets Tessa Metcalfe, the Breast Counsellor,
and talks about losing her breast

Mutilation of any part of the body is always a devastating experience, for it strikes at the heart of who we are, our self image, our sexuality and our sense of personal worth. If loss of a finger or toe makes a person feel incomplete and somehow of lesser worth, how much more costly is the loss of hair, facial integrity, a breast, or part of the genital area. Perhaps one of the cruellest features of cancer is that it so often causes mutilation, changing a person's appearance in a way that threatens their self-esteem.

Malignant *cachexia*, the weight loss which so often accompanies cancer in its terminal phase, makes a man or woman look older and less attractive. The converse of this is seen in the gross weight gain that can occur with long-term steroid therapy or hormone treatment. This is especially tragic in young men or women with brain tumours whose symptoms of headache, sickness, and mental impairment can only be kept at bay by high doses of powerful steroids. It can be heartbreaking to sit with a young husband or wife while they show you photographs of how their spouse used to look before they became ill. You look at radiant wedding or night-out photographs and struggle to realise that the beautiful healthy young person in the photograph is the same as the dull, bloated figure sitting sadly before you. I write about such mutilation and sadness because it is so very important that friends, family, clergy and professional carers of cancer patients have as much understanding as possible of the likely feelings and difficulties of those unfortunate enough to be mutilated in some way. It is only by developing the sort of vision that sees beyond a damaged exterior that all of us can hope to meet and understand the whole person beneath.

Comment on Chapter 10

*In which Katie Roberts meets a kind, forthright doctor –
and a young man with leukaemia.*

There are more women like Liz working in gynaecology these days and I think that is good news for patients, because many women find it easier to talk to another woman about issues of menstruation, intercourse and the various tedious ills that constitute 'women's troubles'. What matters, however, is not the gender of a doctor but their competence, their skill in communication and the sensitivity with which they treat their patients. That all doctors should be competent and diligent is clearly mandatory, but there is another subtler issue: taking patients and their problems seriously.

As a doctor, I know that it is easy enough to take important symptoms seriously but more difficult to be patient and painstaking with symptoms which are clearly unrelated to life threatening disease. Influenza, sinusitis, the common cold, constipation, stress, incontinence, itch, mild depression and anxiety are all debilitating ailments which are not exactly serious but which make life miserable. I think it is fair to say that the good doctors are the ones who, having put themselves in their patient's shoes, set about solving the problems with all the skills at their disposal coupled with a certain dogged tenacity which does not give up the chase before a problem has been solved.

Perhaps that is why it is good for doctors to be ill from time to time because it gives them a much greater understanding of how horrid it is and how completely desperate one can become with what are sometimes considered trivial ailments. I had a hysterectomy last year and found, to my surprise, that my greatest suffering came, not from the psychological impact of losing my uterus, nor yet from the pain of major surgery, but from the utter misery and indignity of being unable to move my bowels! The doctor on duty that day was a kind and gentle man who told me how be valued my books, but I would have traded him gladly for anyone who would have investigated and resolved my constipation. Ah well! Perhaps I needed the experience to teach me to take my own patients more seriously!

How, the reader must wonder, can I write about my own constipation when I should be reflecting about Robbie, and what it must be like to face death by exsanguination at the tender age of 22? Perhaps it is because I, like everyone else, find such premature death so cruel, so terrible, that it is easier to talk about something else. There is, too, the inescapable fact that I simply do not know what it is like to face death at this age, because I have never done it. The character of Robbie is a distillation of all the young cancer patients I have ever met or heard about, and all the fear and despair and pain that I have personally suffered. Ironically, only yesterday, I had to tell a real young man that his leukaemia-like illness had come back. He had just had a massage and was relaxed and happy, so the news, which he had asked for, caught him particularly undefended. It was painful in the extreme to see his smooth young face crumple like a child's as he realised the implications of what I was saying.

The tears ran down his cheeks as he paced my office like a wild animal, hugging to his chest the large teddy bear that lives here. As I watched him weep and listened to him sobbing that he could not face more needles, more sickness, more drug treatment, my heart ached. There were no clever words of reassurance or comfort. All I could do was hug him and then stand there impotently, sharing, in some small measure, his awful pain.

Comment on Chapter 11

In which Mary Carlisle comes round from her operation and, later, meets Oncologist Dr Andrew Radcliffe

For the purposes of this book, I have portrayed Mary as having a particularly aggressive tumour, so that I can discuss the full course of the disease within the time span of the story. It is unusual, though sadly, not impossible for a patient with breast cancer to 'progress' so rapidly. More commonly, there is a disease-free interval of anything from 18 months or so to several years, sometimes more than ten, in which the patient is completely well. When the disease relapses it can do so virtually anywhere in the body, depending upon where the 'secondary' tumours grow. Common sites are the bones, the lungs, the liver and the brain. Once disease has spread the goal of treatment is *palliation*, relief of symptoms, rather than cure. The disease may respond well to a course of chemotherapy or to hormone treatment, so that 'worthwhile' remissions are obtained. A remission is a period of time in which the disease has regressed or is static.

The art of palliative care is the balancing of treatment against unpleasant side effects and quality of life. So, if a particular treatment is very unpleasant and makes the patient feel miserable, it may be that the survival gains achieved are not sufficient to make the treatment worthwhile. Treatment should ideally be tailored to the individual patient, for example, a young mother may be prepared to undergo unpleasant chemotherapy because each day gained is another precious day with her husband and children. An elderly widow, on the other hand may dread her life alone and may refuse treatment to prolong her life. Such treatment must be sensitively negotiated with the individual patient so that any treatment is of their choosing.

This modern concept of a partnership between doctor and patient attacks the roots of the outmoded paternalistic relationship in which the doctor told the patient what treatment they were to have, without explanation or consultation.

Comment on Chapter 12

In which Robbie learns that he has only a few weeks to live

'Breaking Bad News' is a high priority teaching issue in the world of cancer care. In 1980, when I began to work with patients with cancer, it was considered cruel to tell patients the truth about their illness if they could not be cured. Many cancer specialists were deliberately vague in order to shield the patients from the truth, whilst others were quite comfortable about lying outright. 'Just a few little cells which might become cancerous' is a phrase I remember my boss using while he promised to 'chase them away' with his Jungle Juice, the chemotherapy.

Fifteen years on, things are substantially different and it is the norm for patients to be informed of this diagnosis if they ask about it. This is clearly a better situation than before, but there is still much room for improvement in the manner in which people are told about their situation. Research shows that many patients and their families are dissatisfied with the way in which people are told. Many patients and their families are dissatisfied with the way in which 'bad news', particularly news of insurability and impending death, is 'broken'. It is worth looking, therefore, at some of the more common of the complaints about this issue. The commonest complaint that I hear is that the doctor – for it is nearly always the doctor who undertakes this task – was too abrupt, too matter of fact, unfeeling or downright cruel in the way that he or she informed the patient of his or her prognosis. Is this allegation true, and if it is, what is wrong with the doctors who behave so insensitively?

The answer is true, in part, for many doctors lack the skills required to communicate gently and effectively. It is true that some state the facts too boldly and too matter of factly. But it is not true, I believe, that they do not care. In my experience all doctors care to some extent about their patients, for if they did not they would find a less demanding way of earning a living. The problem is not that they do not care but that they care too much and they hide these feelings in the belief that it is unprofessional for a doctor to show feelings. This, is, I believe, one of the saddest situations, because in the long run, what our patients need from us is the knowledge that we care about them, that they are persons of worth. Contemporary poet Sydney Carter, writes:

> No revolution will come in time
> to alter this man's life except
> the one surprise of being loved.

The trouble is, most doctors grossly underestimate the importance of warmth in their interaction with patients, so many of whom are ill at ease and frightened. This human warmth is especially important when bad news is broken because patients are at their most vulnerable and therefore especially in need of Bowlby's 'secure base', the person who will comfort and protect their inner child.

This is not the place to describe in detail how doctors and nurses should communicate, but the following guidelines may be helpful:

1. Bad news should *always* be broken in privacy, not in an open ward with other people listening, and never over the telephone.
2. The carer should be at pains to establish a rapport with the patient and, having found out what she knows about her illness, determine what she wants to know. Some patients do not wish to be informed about their situation; this is their chosen coping strategy and we interfere with it at our peril.
3. Having found that the patient does wish to be told the truth, the doctor should impart his information in a language that the patient can understand, with as much sensitivity as he or she can muster and at a rate determined by the patient. This is called a *patient centred* communication, because the doctor is working not to his own agenda but to that of the patient. By this I mean that the doctor does not deliver a 'speech' about the patient's condition and the treatment he can offer but responds, in a step-wise fashion to the patient's questions. This process takes a little longer than the common practice of delivering a speech (such as 'I'm sorry, Mrs X, but I've got

some bad news for you. Your cancer has come back, but don't worry because we're going to do this and that . . .'). The time spent is infinitely worthwhile, because the patient is worthwhile, because the patient is not only grateful but is much better equipped to face what is happening.

4. When bad news is broken powerful feelings are evoked, feelings which the patient needs to express. Part of the process of this communication, therefore, is allowing the patient to process the information offered and giving them the time and the opportunity to express their fear, anger or despair. When the news we give is painful, the patient's reaction, if he is allowed the space to be himself, will also be painful. He may reject the information as untrue, be angry at what is happening to him or be overcome by grief and burst into tears.

None of these emotions is easy to face; we feel uncomfortable, embarrassed and even afraid. We want to get away as quickly as possible, but ideally we should stay and 'hold' the patient while he struggles to make sense of what is happening to him. What the patient needs at this stage is not a lecture on the likely outcome of his disease or details of the treatment we are offering but our receptive, silent caring, our being there *for* him, our *sharing* of his distress.

Comment on Chapters 13 and 14

In which Robbie talks to his friend and mentor, David Meredith, a Jesuit priest

David's relationship with Robbie is drawn from my own experience of relationships with a number of different priests over the years. I have been particularly lucky to have been supported and guided by some very kind and wise mentors who have listened to me as I have struggled to find my way. If I were facing death I would seek the help of such a person, and I, in my turn, provide such spiritual accompaniments as I am able for the men and women with whom I work.

The spiritual accompaniment of the dying is a delicate task which requires that we find out where each individual patient is both emotionally and spiritually and work with them in that 'place'. We must not give in to the temptation, however pressing, to impose our own belief systems upon them. Different individuals may have different understandings (or none) of God. One will have a very personal relationship with Jesus as friend while another may have a deep sense of a power, 'behind the universe' but little notion of a personal God. What is important, I believe, for those in a pastoral role, is to discern whether or not the individual is troubled by guilt about a particular issue, and help him or her work through things until they achieve a degree of peace.

In this context it is worth drawing a distinction between an individual's *spiritual needs* and his or her religious needs. While only 'religious' people have religious needs, to do with prayer, and ritual, we *all* have spiritual needs. They concern the individual's quest for meaning, the search for an answer to the eternal questions of life. Who am I? Why am I here? Where am I going? What happens after death, and has my life been worthwhile?

Comment on Chapter 15

In which Robbie and Katie have a picnic with David and are taken home to tea with Susie

Is this tale of love on a summer's day too good to be true? I think not. Alice Duer Miller, an American poet, writes powerfully of the experience of lovers under sentence of death:

> We went down to Devon
> In a warm summer rain,
> Knowing that our happiness
> Might never come again;
> I, not forgetting,
>   'Till death do us part',
>   Was outrageously happy
>   With death in my heart.
>
> Lovers in peace time
> With fifty years to live,
> Have time to tease and quarrel
> And question what to give;
> But lovers in wartime
> Better understand
> The fullness of living,
>   With death close at hand.

from 'The White Cliffs', by Alice Duer Miller
[Published by Methuen & Co Ltd., London 1941]

People who work closely with the dying learn to respond rapidly to the moment, to 'seize the day' in order to help their patients live to the full the life that remains. I have vivid memories of a young woman not unlike Katie (although she was terminally ill) languishing in her hospice bed one beautiful afternoon. I tried hard to persuade her to come out of doors with me but she could not summon the strength. Eventually, exasperated, I grabbed her by the hand and led her barefoot down the hospice corridor and out into the car park to a bank full of wild flowers and left her there to pick them!

Inside, I felt a bit sheepish and wondered if I had pushed her too far, until she approached me, windswept and radiant, and presented me with the bunch of flowers she had picked! After that she went out each day to enjoy the summer until the weather failed and she herself was too ill to leave her chair.

When people are dying, one has to strike a balance between risk and safety. One of my wildest and most successful impulses was to take another dying patient into the hospice garden. This young man was much sicker than the girl, but longed to escape the claustrophobia of his single room. Faced with the same sort of logistical problem as the friends of the man in the gospels who was let down through the roof on a stretcher, I summoned the fire brigade who willingly carried my patient down the stairs in his arm chair and laid him tenderly on a sun bed – purchased in haste by his mother – under the apple tree. Looking at his ashen face as he lay there in the spring sunshine, I wondered if he would die there, but I knew that if he did it would have been worth it for the joy it gave him and his parents.

Comment on Chapter 16

In which Joe Peterson develops a peritonitis and his wife, Jeannie, has to cope with getting him to hospital

In this chapter, Joe and Jeannie speak for all the frail, elderly couples whose lives are so cruelly disrupted by accident or illness. There are so many people like Joe and Jeannie in our society, sweethearts and lovers whose bodies have just worn out while their minds and hearts live on. We need to make a special effort to remember that beneath the withered exteriors of the very old there live on the young men and women that they used to be. The beauty queens and the dashing young fighter pilots of the 1940s are, in these closing years of the second millennium, withered like grass, yet still alive, their loves and their memories burning as brightly as they did 60 years before.

Illness in such couples is particularly tragic since it frequently destabilises the frail balance of their domestic situation and forces them to give up their homes and go into care. Another common situation among the elderly occurs when one partner suffers deterioration of their mental faculties. Alzheimer's disease is, in many ways, more cruel than cancer because the body continues to function long after the mind has died. The manner in which many elderly people, or their middle-aged children, care for relatives who are mute and incontinent is nothing short of heroic, but these are the heroes and heroines who remain, as yet, unsung.

Comment on Chapter 17

In which patient Tom Hitchcock meets Jess, Joe and Jeannie Peterson's neighbour

Tom Hitchcock reminds us of the pain of marital breakdown, and the vulnerability and loneliness of single people when they become seriously ill. It is so easy to assume that everyone has a loving family to cherish and care for them when they are convalescent, but this is not always true. People's relationships with siblings, cousins, and so on is not always such that they are welcome to come and stay for several weeks before they are well enough to go home.

I can well remember one bleak February when I was in hospital with an acute attack of asthma. No sooner had I been moved from my grey single room overlooking the hospital's sunless inner well to a bright ward with a glorious view over the moors, than a young doctor came in and told me cheerfully that I could go home the following day! I knew quite well that my chest was better and that they needed the bed but I was close to tears at the thought of being alone in a cold flat, 72 steps up from the street. My glorious attic overlooking the sea is a veritable fortress when I am well, but it now suddenly seemed like a lonely prison where I would die of loneliness and starvation!

All this talk about unreasonable fear and loneliness takes us right back to the concept of attachment theory. When we are sick and in hospital we become as children, dependent upon others for our very survival, so it is hardly surprising that a return to adult independence is not always easy. Tom Hitchcock would have felt like this when it was time for him to be discharged from hospital. Although he had resented his loss of privacy he would have become dependent upon the nurses for help with his colostomy and for company when he felt low.

Jess and Tom clearly became friends after that chance meeting in the hospital, so perhaps she visited him at home after he was discharged. Just how soon he moved in with her history does not relate but one can but rejoice for them in their happiness together.

It is in situations such as these that I find myself questioning the certainty of some churchmen (and women?) when they lay down the rules about human behaviour. How can they be so sure? Should Jess and Tom's relationship remain platonic for ever? Or should they at least have remained chaste until decently married in a registry office? Who knows, for who am I to pronounce upon the ethics of a physically mutilated man and the lonely woman who has learned to love him. And if, as seems likely, Tom remained impotent, would their physical closeness be upsetting to God? I doubt it.

Comment on Chapter 18

In which Robbie dies

The death of a young man, indeed, the death of any young person, is both poignant and distressing. How could it be otherwise? Death from massive haemorrhage is especially hard for the onlookers, although the suffering of the patient is often mercifully brief. My description of Robbie's death is drawn from my experience of the death of a young woman at the hospice where I worked as a doctor for 11 years. It is in moments such as these that hospice staff become totally united and, all differences laid on one side, function perfectly as a team. It is the hidden face of the hospice, the reality behind the bland image and the clichés 'death with dignity' and 'tender loving care'. This is the iron hand in the velvet glove, the competence without which the compassion would be ineffectual.

The 'management' of the actual moment of death is important; not, I believe because it is the climactic moment of an individual's life, but because it is an important legacy for the family, friends and carers. Memories of a 'bad' death may linger for years to torment the bereaved and may interfere with the cherishing of the 'good' memories of the last weeks and days of a person's life. One cannot always predict which death will be 'peaceful' and which will be distressing but as a general rule, death resulting from suffocation or haemorrhage is usually best managed in hospital. I say this because there may be a need for crisis treatment such as is described in Robbie's death. If such deaths occur at home without medical or nursing help available, the carers may be left with feelings of guilt that their care of the dying person was inadequate and that he or she suffered more than was necessary.

It is also worth putting on record that, in leukaemia, a death such as Robbie's, that is by major gastrointestinal haemorrhage, is rare. Death from pulmonary complications of bleeding from the lungs or a cerebral haemorrhage is more common.

Comment on Chapter 19

*In which Community Macmillan Nurse Victoria Woodhouse
visits Joe and Jeannie Peterson*

'

One of my patients once described Macmillan Nurses as 'the best
thing since sliced bread' and I can only endorse his view. These
specialist nurses work in the community supporting the Primary
Care Team[1] in their caring of men and women dying of cancer.
As specialist nurses, they have a narrower focus for their work
than 'district' nurses and thus develop a wide experience and
expertise in caring for patients with cancer, particularly those who
are in the terminal stage of their illness.

These nurses are funded initially by the charity Cancer Relief
and then taken over by the health authority of the district in
which they work.

The Marie Curie nurses, however, are funded for a different
purpose. These provide hands-on support, especially at night, for
cancer patients who are terminally ill. The availability of these
nurses makes it possible for patients like Joe Peterson to be cared
for at home.

The 'management' of Joe's death is clearly different from that
of Robbie's. Joe is dying slowly from the effects of disseminated
bowel cancer. His pain is controlled and he is reasonably comfortable within the confines of his increasing weakness and cachexia.
It is unlikely that there will be any sudden catastrophe requiring
hospitalization, so his care consists in controlling his symptoms,
good nursing care and hygiene, emotional support and the support
of his elderly wife.

Joe and Jeannie are indeed lucky that they have such kind
neighbours. If it were not for Tom and Jess, Jeannie would not be
able to cope and Joe would have had to be admitted to hospital.
By helping Jeannie to care for her husband in their own home,

[1] The GP and his team of Practise Nurses, District Nurses and Health
Visitors are known as The Primary Care Team.

Tom and Jess are enabling Joe to be in his own home until he dies, and giving his wife the opportunity to adjust to this massive change in her life and status.

Despite the availability of Macmillan and Marie Curie nurses, many patients who would like to remain in their homes are unable to do so. This is sometimes because the spouse or children do not feel able to care for the dying person, but more often because the heavy care required means that one nurse is not enough. Only the wealthy can afford to buy nursing care around the clock.

Perhaps one day the Marie Curie organization may expand so that they can offer round the clock nursing, but until then, hospices and hospitals will have to care for those whose families cannot cope with the burden of heavy nursing.

Comment on Chapter 20

*In which Mary and John Carlisle celebrate their last
Christmas together and their doctor, Michael Howard,
discovers that his wife is pregnant*

Perhaps one of the compensations for growing older is that we learn that, for the majority of people, life is a kaleidoscope of ups and downs, heartbreak and joy. Even in the hard times there is often a richness of experience and relationships that could not have been achieved in an easier way. My own life has been particularly rich in this respect. Had I not made friends with a Chilean, I would never have been tortured, never suffered years of post traumatic distress but then neither would I have had my narrow xenophobic horizons expanded and gained so many wonderful friends. If I had had a secure, loving childhood perhaps I would have moved on to form a stable, loving marriage. But the flip side of that is that I might never had known the amazing joy of creation, the unique fulfilment of the writer.

In similar vein, had Father David Meredith not required therapy he would never have met Susie, and if Michael Howard had not narrowly missed losing his wife their love might never had deepened in the way it did.

The other point to be aware of is the 'growth' of our two ladies with cancer. True, Mary is moving inextricably towards her death, but the neurotic, desperate woman of six months before has been replaced by a serene, mature woman, grateful for the life she has been given and devoting her final energies to helping her husband and children adjust to her impending death. Although I have not, for lack of space, recounted the story of how Mary came 'to terms' with her mortality, she did not do it unaided. She was helped first by practice nurse Caroline, by John, her husband, and then by Tessa, the counsellor. When her disease ultimately relapsed, as it did after only a couple of months of chemotherapy, she was referred to Victoria, the Macmillan Nurse. Victoria would have visited Mary weekly or more, throughout the weeks and months of her terminal illness, listening to her, explaining things, relieving anxiety and generally supporting her. She would have worked closely with Dr Howard over both Mary's symptom control and her emotional support, in the pattern of multidisciplinary care which has become the norm in British cancer care.

Katie, too, has clearly grown, her considerable personal resources mobilized by her relationship with Robbie and by the support given to her by David and Susie. Katie's journey inward with Susie is already benefiting her, not least because, in the warmth and security of the therapeutic relationship she is both enabled to face her past and grieve for it and empowered to take control of a life which had hitherto been disastrously at the mercy of her emotions. Like Susie, we may have high hopes for the emergent Katie.

Comment on Chapter 21

In which John Carlisle, depressed following the death of his wife Mary, is visited at home by psychiatrist Chris Walker

Grieving after the death of a close friend or relative is a painful but normal process which may be described under three main headings.

Shock and numbness. Immediately after a death, the bereaved person is frequently in a state of numbness and shock in which they need to be cherished and cared for. The state partially protects the person from the pain of acute grief in a way which may be compared to numbness experienced by those soldiers who, wounded in battle, somehow carry on, almost oblivious to the pain, and cushioned against the reality of their injury.

Acute grief. After 24 to 48 hours, sometimes after the funeral, the numbness 'wears off' and the person experiences the full pain of their loss. This pain classically comes in waves of terrible sadness which overpower the individual, causing him or her to weep or even to cry out. These waves of grief ebb and flow, leaving the person exhausted and desolate. They may be precipitated by reminders of the dead person either from friends, objects or their own thoughts.

Depression and despair. When the tide of acute grief recedes, perhaps after two to three months, the person may be left 'beached' in what seems an interminable and desolate wasteland. They have no cause for joy, nor can they imagine even being joyful again. Life without their beloved spouse, child or friend is empty and meaningless and they can see no reason for living. This state closely resembles depression and, indeed, it may progress to become a depressive illness so that the bereaved person is unable to function and so needs medical treatment.

Some bereaved people become suicidal, and there are a number of deaths by suicide each year. Elderly widowers are particularly at risk. As the months go by, the bereaved person's chronic sadness and inertia normally give way to acceptance of their new situation and recovery of interest in life. At last, there is light at the end of the tunnel, winter gives way to spring, despair to the first flickerings of hope.

It is important to stress that bereavement is a normal human reaction to death of a loved person; the bereaved are not ill, but disabled by sadness and a major disruption of their support systems. Given adequate support of friends and family, most bereaved people will recover their emotional and physical well being within one to two years. Certain people, however, are at greater risk of being disabled by their loss, and may need the help of a bereavement counsellor, usually a specially trained lay person, to process and accept their grief. Among those who are particularly at risk are those with ambivalent relationships with the deceased, those with a previous history of psychiatric illness, the socially isolated and those who have experienced sudden and violent or multiple losses.

A small proportion of the bereaved may develop a pattern of pathological grief and require help from a psychiatrist, psychologist or psychotherapists.

SUGGESTED READING ON BEREAVEMENT
Through Grief: The Bereavement Journey, Elizabeth Collick, Darton, Longman & Todd, in association with CRUSE, 1986.
Grief Counselling and Grief Therapy, William Worden, Routledge, 1985.
The Anatomy of Bereavement, Beverley Raphael, Routledge, 1991.

Comment on Chapter 22

In which Lisa and Jamie Carlisle attend a group for bereaved children

It is only in very recent years that I personally have begun to understand something about the grief of children following the death of a parent, friend or sibling. Children are sometimes, described as 'the forgotten mourners' because they are so often ignored, shut out from the grief of adults who console themselves by thinking that children will get over their loss quickly and that it is better not to talk about it.

The modern understanding of childhood grief is very different from the popular myth. Children are acutely aware of mood changes in those who are close to them and will become confused and anxious if the reasons for weeping, withdrawal or anger are not explained.

Children's understanding of death depends upon their age, for it is only around six years that a child understands about the irreversibility of death. If a young child is told that mummy has gone away or gone to be with Jesus, he or she may think that she will come back and may be devastated when the reality is understood. It is important to remember, too, about the child's propensity to 'magical thinking', that is believing that he or she has magical powers over people and can cause them harm. A child who has said to a parent or sibling 'I hate you! I wish you were dead' may well believe that he or she is responsible for that person's death.

In many situations, a child may be doubly 'bereaved' because their surviving parent is so caught up in his or her own loss, that he or she is quite unaware of the children's grief. Indeed, children may feel that they have to put on a brave face for their parent, and they learn by example, that grief is not something to be talked about but a pain to be endured in silence or buried in the farthest recesses of the mind.

Such 'buried' grief may be dormant well into adult life and

213

then resurface as a cause of depression or other psychological disorder.

How then may bereaved children be helped? What should professional carers be doing to prevent undue suffering and later harm? The answer to this question is easier to write than to do. In essence, we must remember the children, be aware of them, include them in family discussions about a member's illness. They need to know if a parent or sibling is going to die, so that they can ask questions and try to understand what is happening.

It is much better for grieving adults to share their tears with their children, comforting each other as best they can, than to put on a stoical face. Children, like adults, must do their 'grief work' when someone they love dies. They must accept the reality of the loss and experience the pain of grief before they can move on to withdraw their emotional energy from the relationship with the dead person and invest it in new people and ventures. To adapt an ancient Chinese proverb, we can't stop the birds of sorrow from flying over our children's heads, but we can do our best to stop them making nests in their hair.

Comment on Chapters 23 and 24

In which some loose strands are gathered together

So, all's well that ends well! Tom loves Jess, John marries Alice's mother Harriet, and Katie marries Chris. The reader may wonder what happened to Jeannie, after Joe died? Sorry, I forgot to tell you – Jeannie never really got over Joe's death and when, six months later she discovered that she herself had cancer she just 'gave up'. 'I want to be with my Joe,' she would say when Jess tried to tempt her to eat. 'I've had my life. I'm quite ready to go.'

When she could no longer manage to look after herself at home, Jeannie was admitted to the hospice. Jess and Tom offered to care for her in her own home but she was adamant that she didn't want to be a burden on anyone. Although she only lived a few weeks, Jeannie was very happy at the hospice. She made special friends with Tabitha, the hospice cat who would sit every day on the end of her bed, purring gently. Jeannie died peacefully early one evening, as Jess and Tom kept vigil beside her.

'Well,' said Tom, as they walked towards their car in the hospital car park. 'If that's death, I don't think I'm afraid of it any more'.